D0773075

THE PACIFIC ALONE

THE PACIFIC ALONE

The Untold Story of Kayaking's Boldest Voyage

DAVE SHIVELY

FALCON

GUILFORD, CONNECTICUT
HELENA, MONTANA

An imprint of The Rowman & Littlefield Publishing Group, Inc.
4501 Forbes Blvd., Ste. 200
Lanham, MD 20706
www.rowman.com

Falcon and FalconGuides are registered trademarks and Make Adventure Your Story is a trademark of The Rowman & Littlefield Publishing Group, Inc.

Distributed by NATIONAL BOOK NETWORK

British Library Cataloguing in Publication Information available

Library of Congress Cataloging-in-Publication Data available

ISBN 978-1-4930-2681-4 (hardcover)   **33614080776106**
ISBN 978-1-4930-2682-1 (e-book)

∞™ The paper used in this publication meets the minimum requirements of American National Standard for Information Sciences—Permanence of Paper for Printed Library Materials, ANSI/NISO Z39.48-1992.

Printed in the United States of America

for Kristin

Contents

FOREWORD

The Pacific Alone is a well-chosen title, recalling the solitary and precarious nature of a trans-Pacific kayak voyage. But while I paddled my kayak alone, my wife, family, and dozens of active supporters—a shadow crew of sorts—came along in spirit. The emotional trauma of family and friends waiting for news of my arrival was real, and Dave Shively's book skillfully weaves these disparate strands—the angst of padding and waiting—into a coherent story. To enable him to tell this story well, I confided in Dave, trusting him with my journals and sharing my thoughts in a series of meetings beside the ocean, surf and sea breezes keeping the conversations real.

When I read *The Pacific Alone*, every word of Dave's vivid retelling rang true, and I re-experienced the exhilaration and terror I felt when I was on that crossing. I was exquisitely aware that some accidental ship encounter, unexpected weather, a physical injury, any small mistake at all, might end in disaster or death. It was precisely that sense of edginess, though, that made my crossing worth doing. Now when I consider that state of being and read Dave's accounts of other human-powered Pacific crossings, some successful and others tragic, I can only reflect on how fine a line exists between success and failure. Even though I lived this story, reading *The Pacific Alone* provided me with deeper insights into my sixty-four days of living on the edge.

Ed Gillet
San Diego

CHAPTER ONE

The Limit

1° 23' 0.4" North, 78° 50' 27.45" West—
Pacific Ocean off the Ecuador-Colombia border
December 1984

THE IDEA EMERGED FROM THE SWAMPY MANGROVE MUCK OF THE LAW-less borderlands.

Ed Gillet paddled alone a under a half-moon. He followed the glowing V-shaped ripple ahead of his narrow kayak's bow. He kept the undulating point fixed on the dark lump of a distant island. Each stroke ahead flashed neon green as his paddle blades sparked small explosions of tiny bioluminescent reactions in the warm equatorial waters.

"The sea was alive," Gillet recalled, noting sudden bursts as sea snakes would rise from the Pacific's depths, "like lightning illuminating a thunderhead at night."

After such a strike, frenzied sardines would land by the dozen on the deck of the adventurer's solo expedition sea kayak—much less tense a matter than having to shoo the occasional sea snake off of the neoprene spraydeck covering his lap (used to keep water out of the boat). Gillet reveled in the dynamic surroundings and silence only broken by wild and abrupt interludes, the slap of acrobatic Mobula rays leaping and flapping furiously out of the water, or a flying fish smacking into his chest with the subtlety of a baseball thrown at close range.

Mainly though, he needed cooler paddling conditions, the night transit a means to avoid northwest Ecuador's debilitating midday heat. This crossing to Isla de la Plata, twenty-five miles offshore, would also provide a scenic detour in Gillet's extended journey up the entire west coast of South America.

It also helped minimize unnecessary run-ins with local boatmen. Since leaving Chile, the locals seemed to be growing more suspicious and more aggressive in their interactions.

The sight of the lone paddler certainly posed more questions than answers. A nonmotorized boat was strange enough. An overloaded red sixteen-foot decked sliver of a craft, however, was another matter entirely. Especially one helmed by a tall, fair-skinned gringo whipping a succession of uninterrupted strokes across remote corners of the coast at a rapid clip, each twist of the torso bouncing a mangled lock of fiery blond hair.

Through Chile the conversations with local fishermen reflected genuine interest and hospitality, often marked by invitations to share stories over vino, with village visits that led to frequent requests for school presentations, autographs for the children, and interviews with newspapers and radio stations small and large. Through the militarized ports of Peru, the inquisitions became much more abrupt. Between the terrorist threat of the leftist Sendero Luminoso (Shining Path) movement, economic collapse, and inexplicably warmer Pacific waters that had left the fishermen hungry, not to mention an "agitated and paranoid" military, which threatened him at gunpoint several times, Gillet felt like he "was being released from jail," finally reaching what he hoped to be friendlier waters.

Before the Isla de la Plata crossing, a talkative local had issued a cryptic warning to look out for *tiburones* (sharks). But it wasn't until a mere half-mile north of the island that Gillet understood that the threat of *tiburones* wasn't actual sharks, but rather, the nickname given to the motorized wood canoes—narrow twenty-four-foot "nautical workhorses" used for fishing or transporting people and goods between coastal villages by day.

As the sun rose on the transit back from the island, Gillet quickly figured out how the *tiburones* were used by night. With his headlight off to avoid becoming an unnecessary target for flying fish, he paddled into an odd-looking square box wrapped in plastic and nylon cord. Upon closer inspection, pulling the box up on his deck, he figured it held about ten kilos of marijuana. After taking a photo of it with his waterproof Nikonos camera, he threw the bale of dope back out to sea. Wasting no time finishing the rest of the crossing, he stopped to resupply, and reassess, in the nearest busy town of Esmeraldas, Ecuador.

Gillet wondered about his next steps. Alone at a Chinese restaurant in Esmeraldas, worlds away from his home in San Diego, he scribbled in a journal:

"I've arrived at a mental state where this trip means everything to me," he wrote. "I can't imagine stopping now—I feel as though I've paddled forever and I don't want to end this anytime soon."

Gillet, at thirty-three, had added a layer of wiry muscle to his otherwise slender frame. Closing in on five thousand miles paddled in the year to date by working up the western coast of South America from Punta Arenas, Chile (just above the Strait of Magellan), Gillet's resolve had hardened northward with his skills. He had learned how to handle every conceivable sea kayak challenge, from harrowing surf landings in the dark to miles spent grinding into the teeth of fifty-knot gales, and how to do it alone. He'd stayed out of trouble by relying on intuition, as well as a little luck—literally dodging bullets fired by a soldier in Puerto Bayóvar, Peru, as warning shots. He had escaped detection by drug traffickers on his recent crossing to Isla de la Plata, where he inadvertently paddled into the rendezvous drop-point. What he didn't have was money.

He'd long burned through the $7,000 loan to fund this expedition. Three months prior in Lima, he had cashed in his return airline ticket. Without enough money to purchase a flight home, Gillet's sights were still fixed firmly ahead: closing the final five hundred miles to Balboa, Panama. There he hoped to crew a yacht that could perhaps offer passage back to Miami or San Diego. So he squirreled away an emergency eighty dollars and spent the rest on food stocks to fuel his final twenty-five days. His final contact with otherwise disinterested Ecuadorian authorities was in the town of San Lorenzo, "a sweltering banana port a day's paddle from the Colombian border."

With a full load of food supplies, he celebrated Christmas by falling back into his "crepuscular existence," meaning laying low in the midday heat and making miles at dawn and dusk. As he plugged northward again under a pale-blue tropical sky, Gillet entered the maze of mangroves marking an area on his chart peppered by coastal towns with no names, no road access, and no connection to the outside world aside from the "steady parade" of the motorized *tiburones* shuttling villagers through the channels.

Thinking he might connect with villagers to secure a safe place to camp for the night, Gillet paddled in toward a particular community. He immediately had second thoughts. This didn't seem like the typical village getting by on subsistence fishing. "I immediately got the vibe that these were not guys I wanted to meet." A mob he described as "deranged and agitated" emerged from the "clusters of wooden shacks squatting on stilts over the steaming tidal flats." Amassing on the rickety dock, they whistled at him, shouting questions about his "mission" in Ecuador. He turned away and began paddling back out to the mangroves.

Only a few hundred yards out from the "ramshackle village," Gillet heard the starting sputter of an outboard motor: A *tiburon* headed straight for him. He raced toward a side channel. Gillet panicked, not knowing whether to ditch the kayak and take his chances in the jungle, or keep paddling full bore. There wasn't time for either. The dugout was approaching full throttle, lifting its bow to conceal the passengers, though Gillet had already clearly spotted three men and two teenage boys on board.

Prepping for the potential impact, Gillet popped off his spraydeck—perhaps he could roll over and swim away underwater, freeing himself from the collision. The motorized canoe cut the throttle feet from his kayak as the log runners used to stabilize the canoe bumped into Gillet's kayak. When one of the teenagers grabbed for his paddle, Gillet managed to wrestle it free and start paddling off. As the canoe idled along to his right, Gillet noticed the crew's eldest member perching in the middle of the boat, pointing the barrel of a rusty double-barreled shotgun down and away. Gillet guessed he was drunk as "his crossed eyes rolled around his pockmarked face."

The order was direct: "Don't move or we'll kill you," the crazed-looking cross-eyed man told Gillet as he and another of the crew pointed their 12-gauges, asking him to hand over his gun.

Gillet had one thought: "This is it." He had no gun buried in his kayak, though he longed to reach for the stainless steel 4-10 single-shot Snake Charmer shotgun he had left in Chile. Should this exchange escalate anymore, he could only think to calculate "the distance between the sharp edge of my paddle blade and the nearest human throat."

Not believing him unarmed, Cross-eyes bent down to grab Gillet's paddle. Slapping away his hands, the two engaged in a "thrust and parry battle," Gillet holding his ground, but not noticing another member of the boat crew grabbing his fifty-foot safety/swim line, which Gillet used to moor his kayak. "I was hooked on a leash I couldn't cut," Gillet suddenly realized, as the men fired up the boat's outboard motor and began towing him back to the village.

As the boat beached, the younger teenagers grabbed the bow line, dragging Gillet "like a captured animal" inside of his kayak, up the muddy shore of the community. A crowd of two dozen villagers circled around the catch. Cross-eyes pointed the barrel of his shotgun at Gillet. The order was clear: Get out of the boat. Gillet stepped out, feet sinking into the mud. As the crew realized he was not some sort of religious missionary figure, they began rooting through his boat, looking for that gun, or perhaps a radio if he was indeed sent to spy on them. Or, maybe something else of tangible value.

"Where is *la plata* [the money]"?

"I don't have any," Gillet responded in a mostly true admission. Though fluent in Spanish, Gillet could only pick up 85 percent of the conversations firing all around him, some worried about what they should do with him, others unconcerned and only wanting to talk. Was he a threat? Divided, no one seemed to know what to do.

Cross-eyes jabbed his shotgun barrel in Gillet's stomach, telling him that if he didn't have money, he ought to then leave his cameras with the town.

"I couldn't stand the abuse any longer," recalled a desperate Gillet, who reacted. He quickly stepped aside, grabbed the gun barrel and pushed Cross-eyes back. Both were equally surprised as the "drunken bandido," tripped over backwards onto the mud; the shotgun ending up in Gillet's hands. Suddenly the stranger was armed.

The surrounding crew immediately leveled five guns at Gillet's chest. Gillet looked around at the destitute condition of the crew. Betting that this raiding party was as absurd as its unbalanced leader, Gillet handed the gun off to a child standing by, watching the proceedings with impartial curiosity. "I said, 'Hey, this is dangerous, put it somewhere safe.'" The exchange produced a few snickers. The mood changed. The tense air of hostility seemed to loosen.

"Go ahead," Gillet shouted. "Kill me."

In the uneasy silence that followed, Gillet began packing his gear back in his kayak.

"I'm leaving," he announced hoarsely, dragging his boat toward the water. "Are you going to shoot me?"

Swallowing anger, muttering curses, Gillet looked back to make sure no one followed him out of town. Catching his breath, voice gone from an hour of crazed screaming, he tried to collect himself in the mangroves. Still shaking, silent in his boat, he looked at his surroundings, unable to paddle forward. "It opened my eyes to the reality that I was in a very dangerous place," Gillet recalled, coming to grips with just how vulnerable and defenseless he was.

Perhaps this was providence, how everything was meant to fall into place. He had gone as far as safely possible. It was time to go home.

Returning to the naval outpost in San Lorenzo, Gillet sold off his kayak, along with his waterproof paddling jacket, tent, and sleeping bag to the *comandante* and his sailors to fund transportation via a rickety military transport plane and bus to Quito. Finally, after trading away his camera to a pair of drunk travel agents still open on New Year's Eve, he had his one-way ticket north to Miami. With the travel arranged, and momentum shifted homeward, he began to reckon with reality. He had fallen short of his goal. He processed the range of emotions: anger at the hostility he had experienced; frustration with having to endlessly explain himself to bureaucrats; and disappointment mostly, not ending the expedition on his own terms.

He needed a new trip. But not something along a coast. "I was confident that I could travel almost anywhere in the world and successfully tackle an unknown coast," Gillet said. Another coast would merely be "ringing changes on the same notes." The plane landed abruptly to refuel—the result of a labor strike and fuel shortage in Ecuador—in, of all places, Panama. Gillet laughed at the irony, having arrived in a roundabout way at his original destination. But the circumstances, with the strike, the close-call kidnapping, all the extra variables told him exactly what he required of a new adventure. He needed a trip as far away from people as possible. A truly solo trip. That is, he needed a trip offshore to "the emptiest place I could imagine."

As he flew home over the blank expanse of the Gulf, Gillet started thinking about possible extended crossings of interest: Isla Guadalupe,

150 miles off the west coast of Baja; Cocos Island, 340 miles off the Pacific shore of Costa Rica; or, the Galapagos Islands, perhaps, a full 565 miles out of his old holiday haunts in Esmeraldas, Ecuador.

But then he considered the cost: The return travel fare, as well as the time and logistics involved. It just stung too much, especially the Ecuador option—getting all the pieces right back to where he just had sold everything to leave?

What if he could essentially leave from his front door—no planes, no permits. And if he was already planning to subsist for days offshore, why not go for the big one?

Why not paddle to Hawaii?

Chapter Two

Katie and the Kayak

37° 42' 28.32" North, 123° 4' 15.42" West—
Southeast Farallon Island
October 1985

THE FOG CLEARED AT DAWN TO REVEAL THE ISLAND'S JAGGED OUTLINE
ahead. Ed Gillet plugged rapid strokes through steely, rolling swell. He
thought little of reaching his goal: the largest of the forbidding cluster of
uninhabited crags twenty-seven miles beyond the Golden Gate.

Rather than fixing attention on the gathering mass of gulls flapping
overhead to the great whites surely lurking below, or the fearless elephant
seals mouthing at his kayak, Gillet was still occupied with thoughts of the
woman back on shore.

She appeared on the Sausalito beach where he and his friend Larry
Robinson prepped their kayaks the prior morning for this marathon day
of paddling. A beige, white-topped '74 Volkswagen bus had pulled into
the parking lot, rack loaded with a twenty-two-foot double rowing shell.
From it, Gillet recalled, "a strikingly tall, strong-looking blonde woman"
emerged, who then approached and sized him up.

"Could I sweet-talk you into helping me unload my rowing shell?"
she asked. "It's 160 pounds and you look like you can hold up your end
of the boat."

Was that a sexist comment? Gillet wondered, though he was quick
to help the woman, who did not mince her direct words. As the pair
unloaded the shell onto the rowing club's storage racks, she explained how
she had raced it with a partner the previous day, and Ed told her of his
plans to kayak the next. She returned to her van, but sensing shared inter-
ests, Gillet grabbed for a magazine he'd brought along on his road trip up
the West Coast. He presented an article through her driver-side window
to keep the conversation going. The story pictured a bearded kayaker and
something about South America.

"Oh, huh, he seems interesting," she said.

"That's me!" Gillet exclaimed.

She did a double-take to the quick, clean-shaven man before her with
"charming reddish-blond hair." Katie Kampe introduced herself, and the
two connected as Gillet downplayed the trying five thousand miles of his

South American epic. Before Katie drove away, Ed, in his nonchalant way, added a mention of his plans to kayak to Hawaii. Somehow, she didn't seem so impressed.

Hawaii aside, a paddling expedition to the Farallon Islands alone was not some kind of gimme. To Gillet, "It was just a thing to do; it's there and it's nice to have an interesting goal," he said. "It's also illegal to land there—and sometimes the goal needs to be sort of illegal to make it fun and interesting because you are doing something that violates what normal people do." To members of the San Francisco paddling community, like Dr. Creig Hoyt, kayaking to the Farallons, a feat that would require over twenty-four hours of sustained paddling, was certainly not something that normal people did. In fact, it was groundbreaking. Prior to Gillet and Robinson, no sea kayakers had ever rounded "The Devil's Teeth."

"We thought it was such an outrageous notion, it wasn't even on our radar screen," Hoyt remembers of hearing the news, which sparked an unofficial race among locals to repeat the feat. "[Gillet] just said, 'Oh yeah, we went out and came back in, it was kind of fun.' And we thought, 'Well shit, if he can do it, so can we.'" The next year, Hoyt and three other locals replicated the circumnavigation in tandem kayaks, a run that thirty years later functions as a badge of achievement when Hoyt's neighbors introduce him as "the guy who kayaked around the Farallons."

In the early '80s, boundaries were constantly being broken. Hoyt's houseboat in Sausalito was a crash pad for seafaring adventurers from across the West Coast converging on San Francisco Bay. It was a tight community of like-minded paddlers. The sport of sea kayaking was still in its preliminary stages of development, far from a mainstream outdoor activity of the masses.

"If you saw someone on the road, with a boat, you knew who it was—that's how small is was," says Bob Licht, who recalls Dr. Hoyt as "one of the central characters" in the Bay Area's tight-knit paddling community. Licht had started his sea kayak outfitting business three years prior with a single boat. By 1985 that sparse community was growing, as was Licht's outfit, Sea Trek. Located on the Sausalito beach where Ed and Katie met, Sea Trek quickly emerged as one of the sport's early West Coast footholds outside of the Pacific Northwest manufacturing nexus between Seattle and Vancouver.

"The reason for the blossoming of sea kayaking during the '80s was because it was still a 'freedom activity,'" says John Dowd, a Kiwi transplant to British Columbia who literally wrote the book on sea kayaking after opening Ecomarine, the world's first specialty sea kayak shop founded on Vancouver's Granville Island in 1980. As backpacking gained momentum, the appeal of another new way to escape urban life also began gaining popularity.

"It was all about packing and going on long trips, so all the boats reflected that," says Licht, who did an extended 1982 road-cycling journey north to visit Dowd and learn the mechanics of operating a shop and guiding shorter sea kayak day tours.

On Gillet and Robinson's super day tour out to the Farallons, they looped down from Point Reyes to the islands, and then straight back east into the bay. That's as much paddling as one could pack into a day. After a midnight start, and fifty-five miles of busy open-water paddling over eighteen hours—in which they opted not to land illegally, exit their boats, and stretch their legs on the island's research facility—they crossed underneath the Golden Gate on an ebbing sundown tide. There, back on the beach, Ed ran into Katie again.

The chance encounters stuck with Gillet as he and Robinson continued up the West Coast, on a pilgrimage, much like their friend Bob Licht's, to sea kayaking's Seattle area hotbed. The soon-to-be stalwart West Coast Sea Kayak Symposium was entering its second year in Port Townsend, Washington. Gillet had been invited to present a slideshow on his South America expedition while Robinson was looking to promote Open Passage, one of the first sea kayaking outfitters to open in Southern California.

On the return trip, the pair routed back through the Bay Area for Sea Trek's big event: the ten-mile race around Angel Island. "The beach fronting Richardson Bay was buzzing with racers and spectators milling around a hundred or so kayaks," Gillet recalled of the scene. As he sat on the grass, contemplating his race strategy through the tidal currents, he heard an unmistakable noise over the crowd. It was the unmistakable high-pitch hoot of Mike Neckar, "a huge, barrel-chested guy who exudes geniality and good humor."

The Czech emigrant to Vancouver was, as Licht put it, holding court. "He was very influential," Licht says. "He was loud and took up a lot of space." That influence had much to do with Neckar's sea kayak designs under his manufacturing label, Necky Kayaks. Referred to in one history of sea kayaking's early days as "the 8,000-pound gorilla in the room," Neckar designed kayaks that had a sexier appeal. These were not cumbersome expedition kayaks, or outsized "folding" wooden-frame Kleppers. They were faster and featured a less rounded, more defined chine (where the hull bottom transitions to the boat's sides). "They were more fun to paddle," says Licht. "And we wanted boats that could handle the conditions we had here, which was chop, and by far, his boats would perform better. I would give Neckar credit for taking the sport from more than just big expedition kayaks."

When Ed Gillet saw the kayak that Neckar had brought down to the Sausalito beach that day, it was exactly the big expedition boat that he had in mind. Neckar's new creation was a tandem kayak he had christened the Tofino, "named for the pretty port in Clayoquot Sound on Vancouver Island's western shore," Gillet recalled, "with a five thousand-year-old paddling tradition, and a favorite destination for modern sea kayakers."

Gillet knew that his kayak for the Hawaii expedition would need to meet a few basic criteria. The first was internal storage. Only a tandem kayak would have space for food, water, and gear, plus enough available space to sleep inside. But Gillet doubted the longer hull of a tandem would hold up to the constant demands of an extended offshore trip, "where rough water survival was paramount." He needed performance with size. He also needed speed. The folding kayaks used by Hannes Lindemann in 1956 and Franz Romer in 1928 for their famed transatlantic crossings, both of which relied heavily on a single-masted sail, were too wide and too slow of an option for Gillet's liking. The ideal kayak Gillet had in mind did not yet exist.

Then he heard Neckar, and saw his Tofino. For the second time in a week, on the same beach he had just met Katie, once again, "It was love at first sight." The attraction was instant. She was twenty feet long, thirty-one inches wide, pretty standard for a tandem, but "what distinguished the Tofino from other tandems on the market was the increased volume and rocker in the forward hull sections." Translation: tough, seaworthy capabilities, with enough room for two months' worth of food. It looked like "it was designed for surfing down big swells at high speed." Too good to be true. Gillet honed in on the kayak and flipped it over, thinking how much the hull resembled the shape of the slender, bottle-nosed minke whale, as he put it, "a paragon of efficiency."

Most importantly, it was already built. Gillet didn't exactly have funds to finance the construction of a custom craft. He was scraping together gigs delivering sailboats and working as a salvage diver in San Diego Bay. He didn't have C-suite connections to parlay into corporate sponsorship that might bankroll a hatched wonder-craft with every latest technological offering. The only way that Ed Gillet was going to get to Hawaii was on the cheap. This was going to be a stock venture, purchased right off the shelf.

Not that Gillet didn't have his own ideas on how to improve Neckar's stock Tofino—mainly through the addition of a more robust composite layup. Inlaid sheets of Kevlar would result in a stronger deck to allow Gillet to crawl around and distribute his gear load.

Gillet introduced his particular set of needs to Neckar. When he noted how the Tofino looked like the perfect kayak for his plan to paddle to Hawaii, Neckar thought, surely, he must be joking.

"He laughed his hooting laugh until his side hurt," Gillet said, before "swallowing hard, when he realized I was dead serious."

So Gillet upped the ante, offering to order a Tofino, that is, if the standard fiberglass shell could be reinforced. Neckar agreed. "He said, 'OK, I build you Hawaii Tofino,'" Gillet said, "grabbing my hand in his bear's paw grip to seal the deal."

Though he had finally found a suitable kayak, Gillet didn't know then that his business in sleepy Sausalito was far from over. His path and Kampe's continued to overlap. "We ran into each other at breakfast in Fred's Café in Sausalito," Kampe said, "and we seemed to keep running into each other, incidentally." Gillet found out more about this woman so seemingly unimpressed with his plan to cross the Pacific: Daughter of a

US Army Silver Star colonel who served in three wars, she grew up on the move—skiing, playing competitive tennis, riding horses, crisscrossing bays from Chesapeake to San Francisco in sailboats with her father, the career officer, as she moved with her family from coast to coast. Her parents were accomplished sailors, completing the Transpac race from the mainland to Hawaii, raising a competitive rower who would go on to claim an open-water national title. Kampe understood the need to be on the water and wasn't afraid to take a risk.

The two stayed connected as Gillet moved up to Seattle to pursue a book project about his South America adventures, pulling on the threads of a long-distance relationship. Gillet's publisher went under while the initial sparks from Ed and Katie's series of run-ins began to fade. In the summer of 1986, Kampe left the Bay Area and headed south to be with Ed in San Diego.

Ed and Katie rented an apartment in Point Loma, on the west side of the San Diego Bay. Kampe, with her degree in accounting, launched a small rowing business in a twelve-hundred-square-foot shop space a few blocks from Shelter Island. Though the shop sold rowing shells, Ed insisted they also rent out kayaks. With an investment from John Dowd to establish a US partner / southern satellite to Dowd's original Ecomarine location in British Columbia, the shop was soon morphing into a specialty kayak retailer and outfitter. Mike Neckar, the Northwest's other big player in the sport, offered Kampe a favorable deal to stock the shop with some of his Necky Kayaks on consignment terms, which also offered Gillet a chance to check in on the status of his reinforced Tofino order.

By the time the Tofino arrived, summer had passed, though a new emerging class of paddlers were starting to stop by the shop to outfit paddling excursions. Though Ed was still supplementing the shop revenues by diving in the harbor to clean off boat hulls as the weather cooled, he and Katie were still strapped for cash, "So we hired out my Tofino for the rest of that year to help pay for the boat." When the boat wasn't being rented out, Gillet "stole whatever time" he had to work on the Tofino between hours in the shop and, increasingly, hours on the water, offering kayak instruction and leading short trips.

"Every single day he did one small thing to further the trip," Kampe said.

"I lay awake at night running 'thought experiments' on the best way to outfit my boat," Gillet recalls. The deck still needed more strength, so Gillet reinforced it with aluminum plates. He needed more internal space, so he removed the bulkhead wall separating the front and rear passenger cockpits. That opened a six-foot-long cavity that would constitute his cockpit by day and cabin by night. Next up, the rudder seemed problematic, "Too weak for my taste." He replaced the stock rudder pin with a more robust "bombproof" steel bracket assembly that a machinist friend named Steve Young connected to a two-foot-long, one-inch-thick Lexan blade. After he had reinforced Young's steering mechanism, Gillet was satisfied with the rest of Neckar's system, which linked the rudder blade via steel cables to a pair of foot pedals.

The next modification was a little trickier to accept, especially given these reinforcements. Gillet needed to drill a hole in the hull. The 2.5-inch-diameter hole could access a small paddle wheel, the spinner providing an instantaneous speed readout on a battery-operated knot-meter he installed in the cockpit. He couldn't figure a better way to determine an efficient pace in such a large kayak. This was years before readily available and affordable handheld GPS units, and the knot-meter would provide necessary estimates of his position and drift on ocean currents. "The tandem boat was so big and heavy that it was impossible to feel tiny speed fluctuations," Gillet said. "Over the distance I would travel, changes of a tenth knot could make a difference of several days to my transit time." That still left a gaping through-hull hole that Gillet meticulously coated in fiberglass to fix it in place and prevent leakage.

Some of the necessary open-ocean gear that Gillet began to stockpile was familiar from his years spent sailing: radar reflector, safety harness, compass, VHF radio, and a high-volume diaphragm bilge pump that he rigged up with a hose through the deck. Other items, however, required extra thought, and real experiments, for how to customize the craft for the sheer physical task of paddling a six hundred-pound payload stuffed inside a twenty-foot tube. How would he store water? How would he rig a sea anchor? How would he stabilize the boat at night otherwise? How would he stay dry inside the kayak?

The last question—protection from the elements—Gillet thought to remedy by constructing a bullet-shaped fiberglass hood. At night, the hood would be utilized to cover the top of the rear cockpit, from which he was planning to paddle during daylight hours. He fixed a rubber gasket on the outside of his cockpit rim and glued rings on the inside of the hood. It all appeared to function: Just pull the lid shut and use some nylon cord attached to the rings to tie the lid closed. He could test it later.

For water storage, Gillet found a twenty-five-gallon collapsible Hypalon rubber water tank. He figured that at eight pounds per gallon, the extra two hundred-some pounds would be like the equivalent of another paddler, but having a reserve would be key, should something go wrong with filtering water. And how to filter seawater? Again, with no money to spend, Gillet started calling in favors, starting with a loaner Seagold reverse-osmosis pump that would have set him back a couple thousand dollars.

Of course, the biggest favor to call in was from Katie. Gillet needed a serious amount of time away from the couple's start-up business, renamed Southwest Kayaks in March 1987. In April, a month after the new shop was up and running, Ed asked Katie to marry him.

"I said, 'Yes,' and his face fell," Kampe recalls, laughing. "It's like, 'Ahh crap. OK. Now what do we do?'"

Finances were tight and it was a second marriage for them both.

"I looked through the Yellow Pages and I called Anytime Marriage Service." Kampe can still picture the details down to the look of their officiant-for-hire who showed up a couple of weeks later with "spiked blonde hair, pink blouse, blue suit, pink handbag, and pink shoes." Katie and Ed each tabbed a friend to join them at Torrey Pines State Park for a short ceremony at an overlook with sweeping views out over the Pacific. Kampe's parents drove down from the Bay Area and toasted the new couple at a fancy seafood feast afterward. For a honeymoon, Katie and Ed loaded up the VW bus and headed south of the border.

Their Mexico getaway did not involve relaxing with piña coladas by the pool. Instead, Gillet and Kampe headed to Canyon Tajo, a remote rock-climbing destination. Thinking of the finger-jamming moves ahead, the newlyweds took off their wedding bands and left them behind in the van's ashtray. Ed led the way as the couple billy-goated over boulders on the precipitous approach to a three-pitch climb that offered open views north all the way to the Salton Sea. Reveling together at the top of the climb, they couldn't see the passerby who picked through the parked van below—and walked away with the wedding rings.

Gillet's sights were still fixed west, on an experience at sea he would later call "the most difficult trip I could conceive of surviving." Much like this honeymoon adventuring on the frontier-lands of northern Mexico, Ed had devised a plan of action, and Katie was game to follow at his side. He even asked her if she'd be interested in joining him in the Tofino to Hawaii. "That took me zero seconds to answer," she laughs. "OK, maybe one. I said no."

Most husbands would not even get up the gumption to ask, let alone expect, the blessing, to go alone—a month after their marriage, saddled with a new business venture heading into its busiest summer months. To Katie however, it wasn't that crazy a request.

"You have got to understand my father and my heritage," she explains, pointing to a vivid moment as a junior high student, watching from the White House Rose Garden as President Johnson awarded her father, Ray, the Medal of Honor. She grew up hearing the colonel's stories about each of the three times he'd been shot in combat, jumping out of planes into Nazi-occupied Germany, storming and holding hills in Korea, managing the First Cavalry Division air mobile and attached units in Vietnam. "He was a force," she says. "You had to be to do what he did, as a maverick who worked his way up the ranks."

Meanwhile, Katie's mother, Peg, was no stranger to maintaining calm during chaos. On the windswept open ocean beyond San Francisco Bay, the family would often bundle together in waterproof all-weather gear during outings in a Cal 20. Later when the couple competed in the Transpac race, launching forty-two-foot sailboats from the Presidio Yacht Club under the Golden Gate, Col. Kampe would join Peg on her watch as she steadied both the lurching boat and the colonel's constant intensity, singing as she sailed. "She would be humming," Kampe remembers of her mother, "sailing down twenty-foot swells."

"So, my heritage says, of course Ed can paddle to Hawaii," she says. "How hard can it be?"

CHAPTER THREE

The Distance

Neither Ed Gillet nor anybody else, to his knowledge, had any idea how hard paddling a kayak from California to Hawaii could be. Or whether it was even possible.

For an expedition of this scale, Gillet did not have any frame of reference. He had heard nothing of previous human-powered attempts to cross the void between the West Coast and the Hawaiian Islands. There was no Internet in 1987. There were no stories circulating of the two navy pilots' 1974 survival voyage in a Zodiac raft; no knowledge gleaned from Patrick Quesnel's four attempts to row the stretch between 1972 and 1976; no warnings from the crew in British Columbia who in 1978 launched a *Kon-Tiki*-like shot at the crossing in a dugout sailing canoe. The only paddler that Gillet knew of who had tackled a similar trans-ocean distance was Hannes Lindemann, and the book on the German adventurer's 1956 crossing of the Atlantic—in a Klepper sailing kayak at that—was not published until 1993.

The only context Gillet had for grueling unknown paddle-powered crossings, he picked up directly from fellow expedition sea kayakers. In the Sausalito circle around Sea Trek, he crossed paths with accomplished and outspoken British sea kayaking instructor, author, and boat designer Derek Hutchinson, who told Gillet of his two attempts to cross "a hundred miles of the most unpredictable sea in the world" on the North Sea crossing from England to Belgium. After leading an expedition that ended in rescue after thirty-four punishing hours of nonstop paddling, Hutchinson returned with two others in 1976 to set a then world record for distance traveled in a sea kayak.

"Derek said that he and his partners felt they were breaking barriers with their North Sea crossing," Gillet recalls. "No one they knew had ever paddled so far and for so many hours in single kayaks. They were not sure if it was even possible for them to endure the hardships they would experience on their crossing."

Could he accomplish a trip much more aggressive than Hutchinson's? The only way Gillet could gauge his capability was through the lens of his prior long-distance paddling experiences.

31° 01' 32.8" North, 114° 49' 52.7" West—
Gulf of California, San Felipe, Mexico
November 1981

Ed Gillet's first kayak excursion was more than a tour around San Diego Bay. More, as in 680 miles down the eastern Gulf coast of the Baja California peninsula. In 1981 Gillet was working in San Diego Bay cleaning the bottoms of sailboats between rock climbing trips up to the big walls of Yosemite and northern Baja. He worked out a trade for some big-wall gear to clean off the hull of a boat belonging to Ray Jardine. The climbing pioneer, inventor of the ubiquitous Friend camming device, and early proselytizer of light and fast alpinism extended an invite to Gillet to join him on a paddling expedition down the Sea of Cortez.

"We made our rudders in the van driving down," Gillet remembers of the jerry-rigged fourteen-foot downriver kayaks, noting his plan to use a "little piece of webbing around my big toes to try and steer." For paddles, they used closet poles with laminated sheets of newspaper fiberglass-ed flat on either end for blades.

Gillet had never been in a kayak. And though he had logged thousands of miles sailing offshore at that point, he noticed something different that November morning when he launched from San Felipe, Mexico, and attached his toe straps. There was no noise like that of a typical sailboat, only "the raspy good-bye kiss of the beach on my thin fiberglass hull." Gillet described immediately feeling "as comfortable on the water as if I had been born there," captivated by the silent, simple, and slender craft, "moving forward as natural as breathing," as though he could go on paddling forever.

"I half-expected to see him shipwrecked," Jardine wrote of Gillet's turbulent maiden launch through the surf. "Finally, about 300 yards out I turned, and with great relief saw Ed coming on strong. I thought: 'this fellow has potential.'"

"I didn't know how or where my journey would end and I didn't care," Gillet wrote, "as long as I kept moving forward I felt satisfied."

Though the journey with Jardine did come to an end in La Paz, three weeks and 680 miles later, Gillet was not deterred. Regimented thirty-mile days, often spent painfully paddling the crude homemade gear, did not shake his resolve; Gillet had encountered an addictive new realm of consciousness propelling himself forward on the water.

Gillet set his sights further. He looked north to the Inside Passage. The thousand-plus miles stretching through a network of islands from Puget Sound up to the Alaska Panhandle had long offered ships and ferries a navigable north-south waterway largely protected from the open ocean. North America's burgeoning class of sea kayakers had a benchmark coastal journey to safely stretch miles into wild and pristine surroundings.

Jardine wasn't interested in joining Gillet, who enlisted help from a local San Diego kayak builder named Joe Sedavic to help him craft a larger boat for the longer trip. Like Mike Neckar, Sedavic was also a Czech expat steeped in the world of whitewater slalom and downriver kayak racing. In exchange for stories that Gillet would publish about the Inside Passage expedition, Sedavic offered to build him a sea kayak. The only problem was that he didn't have a sea kayak mold. So Sedavic made one inside out, meaning that he fiberglass-ed over a foam plug, similar to how a custom surfboard is formed.

"It was the ugliest boat on the outside that you could imagine," Gillet recalls, "but smooth as a baby's butt on the inside."

With the prototype eyesore rigged to the roof of his VW bug, Gillet rallied twenty-four hours straight up the coast to Seattle. His nerves began building, wondering about paddling the odd shell of a boat (built with no bulkheads) across all that distance—roughly double the length of the Sea of Cortez. On the ferry ride north from Seattle to Juneau, Gillet met Randel Washburne, then a seasoned sea kayaker and budding guidebook author, who reassured him about the safety of the trip. However, on a private charter across Icy Strait to his Glacier Bay launch, Gillet's confidence was shaken again. After having to tie the kayak down over the transom of the fishing boat, rough waters bounced the boat violently, cracking the stern section off the kayak.

As he patched the fiberglass over fire in a rainy campsite of the national park, Gillet took stock of his preparation. Having looked at NOAA weather reports, consulted accurate charts, cruising guides, and tidal current predictions, he knew his surroundings well. The summer season reduced the risk of storms and traffic on the channels, traversed by countless fishing boats, float planes, and ferries—thus limiting the exposure if something went wrong, if say, his stern section broke off.

Sure enough, the longer crossings were "pretty benign." He dealt with the bugs, was never bothered by the bears, caught a few salmon along the way, and enjoyed the view as the twelve hundred miles slipped by over fifty-five "really idyllic" days typically filled by eight solid hours of simply listening to his AM-FM radio, and paddling. As he navigated through the Ballard Locks up into Seattle's Lake Washington, Gillet realized that he had acquired a taste for a certain type of paddling on the trip.

"It cemented the idea that I wanted to make lots of miles," Gillet said. "After the trip, I wrote about two kinds of paddlers: sea otters who sit in one place and chase their tails, building saunas on the beach, setting up a basecamp somewhere and paddling around putting out crab pots; and dolphins, the people who want to make miles, who have this migratory urge. It's kind of like the difference between through-hikers on the Pacific Crest or Appalachian Trail, and PCT/AT people who are weekend day-hikers or car-campers."

Gratified with his ability to cover miles, Gillet's success in reaching Seattle only strengthened his resolve to stretch further. And that need to extend personal benchmarks of possibility drew him to the greatest influence on his paddling life: Steve Landick.

In 1982 Landick was well on his way to establishing his legacy as one of paddling's iconic distance-shattering pioneers. He was two years into what he and expedition partner Verlen Kruger had superlatively dubbed the Ultimate Canoe Challenge, in hopes of courting sponsorship. Their 28,043-mile route crisscrossed the continent, down the Mississippi, up the Atlantic coast and through interior waterways all the way to the Arctic Ocean in Tuktoyaktuk, Northwest Territories. The journey began earning its storied reputation as "the longest canoe journey ever" and living up to its "ultimate" billing with the return leg back to Landick's and Kruger's Michigan homes: down the length of the Pacific coast then up the Sea of Cortez, working inland by voyaging back *up* the Colorado River, through the Grand Canyon.

Gillet was still largely unknown, though with his solo trip that summer down the Inside Passage, Gillet had just covered much of the same Pacific ground as Landick and Kruger. Plus, he spoke Spanish. "Through the kelpvine," he got word Landick might be keen for some paddling support, sea-tripping alone after taking a three-week break in Long Beach to grieve the loss of his newborn child. Meanwhile, Kruger continued south with a new female partner, Valerie Fons, who he had met earlier in their Pacific voyage.

"Steve showed impressive grit and determination in rejoining the effort," said Gillet, who contacted Landick about joining his late-fall paddle down the Pacific length of Baja California. "But he seemed to me to paddle in a stoic, obsessive way, like a burned-out runner at the end of a long race."

Landick, a lean and humble former Navy SEAL, certainly brought a marathon runner's mental edge to the distance. "Paddling with Steve was a grueling affair," Gillet said. "He felt more comfortable paddling his kayak than sitting on the beach with his demons, so we kept moving at all costs, camping only when necessary."

When ocean conditions deteriorated, morale flatlined and Gillet reached physical breaking points; he recalled looking over to Landick, still smiling and in good spirits. This new paradigm of pain wasn't all that Landick introduced. His on-the-move regime meant long days and—suddenly a new necessity—nights in the boats, in order to cover fifty- to ninety-mile sections between protected landings.

They developed a system where Landick would deploy a sea anchor off his bow to slow his sea canoe's drift and to orient his boat's nose into the wind. Gillet would then tie the nose of his kayak off the back of Landick's, and finally end the chain with a kite off his kayak stern to catch the wind and keep the two of them in line with the wave action.

"He was game for anything," Landick said, noting the ease of paddling with Gillet, working out mutual game plans. One aspect of this rigged-together sleeping system that Landick wasn't sure of, however, was what Gillet would do if he flipped over.

"I was always kind of amazed at Ed," Landick said. "For one thing, I don't even think he had a seat in that boat—he was just sitting on a piece of foam, and in order to sleep in that darn thing it was a real act of contortion to get his head down and feet forward to get his head back behind the cockpit. That's one thing about Ed though—I always thought he had a very high tolerance for being uncomfortable."

If there was ever a time Gillet was out of his comfort zone, it was the final 155-mile push from Bahia Magdalena to Cabo San Lucas, across the crashing surf of Todos Santos.

Of the envelope-pushing section, Gillet later journaled: "It's a new moon night and we've been paddling for 40 nonstop hours. The Baja coast, three miles away, is a black presence under a dark sky, a serpentine silhouette as much felt as seen. Before this trip I never believed that I could spend so many hours in my kayak in a routine way. Now there are 16 hours to paddle before I can stretch and walk and run free again. . . . As we glide overhead, startled fish leave ghostly green pinwheels. Arms low to conserve strength, we paddle on. My stroke is so integral to my consciousness I paddle even in my dreams. Steve and I keep track of each other through sidelong glances. Except for the times one of us, bone-weary, slumps and dozes for a few seconds, we keep the same pace side by side, each lost in his own thoughts."

In retrospect, Gillet could recognize the magic in that trancelike state of exertion, what he called an "addicting cocktail of adventure, commitment, and fatigue." That contrary mixture of aware presence with wandering thoughts is where he wanted to live. That mental place, of course, required being grounded in the right amount of discomfort, exposed at one's physical limit.

Moments in the extended transit up the South American coast brought him back to that evasive limit, though only as sips of that "addicting cocktail." It arrived in small doses, before having to return to a camp, crash through the surf, and regroup each night, or in all the wrong quantities, with a bandit's crazed shotgun leveled at him on a muddy flat—ultimately leaving a bad taste in his mouth.

Maybe he just needed a stronger version of the original cocktail. Adventure, commitment, fatigue: With ten thousand miles of sea kayaking experience to his name, he had a deep understanding of all the ingredients. Confidence bolstered on the trip down the Inside Passage, he had learned to manage challenges alone. He had expanded his daily paddling output to a marathon-level threshold, overnighting in the kayak alongside Landick during their monthlong nine hundred–mile expedition. And then he had extended his solo voyaging abilities up the largely unknown coast of South America.

He had all the means to get back to that end—that heady high, synching paddle stokes to consciousness while physically pushing himself to the brink. All he needed was the missing ingredient: a new brink.

CHAPTER FOUR

Departure

36° 36' 08.9" North, 121° 53' 26.1" West—
Monterey Bay Harbor
June 1987

TO GILLET, THE HAWAII CROSSING WAS NO DIFFERENT FROM HIS PREVI-
ous trips—just longer.

He scheduled forty days away from Katie and the kayak shop—forty-
five, tops. It was just another matter of covering a decent amount of miles
each day, and managing a little misery to link those days. And of the
forty-some days, the first few would be the most critical in his need to get
offshore. Prevailing wind and current conditions would impede a bearing
directly west, away from the California coast. Any progress in the volatile
seas and likely headwinds would be mostly south, down far enough to
latitudes where prevailing conditions would shift winds reliably to his
back. Reaching the trade winds there, blowing strongly from a northeasterly direction, would, in theory, whisk him west and slightly south to the
islands.

Gillet's low-budget ideal would have been to paddle straight out of
San Diego Bay. But to calibrate the best launch, he needed to consider
the route more carefully. Though the easternmost point of the Hawaiian Island chain lies just over two thousand miles west of the mainland
United States, and roughly twelve hundred miles south, the route there
utilizing the eastern North Pacific's prevailing winds and currents is far
from a direct A-to-B vector as the crow flies (or, say, the ocean-crossing
golden plover).

The primary factor is the California Current. Considered a subtropical boundary current, the California Current runs south, reacting to the
ocean basin "boundary" of the North American continent, moving cold
Alaskan water down along the West Coast toward the equator. This
southward flow, which extends hundreds of miles offshore, then enters
the tropics off the coast of southern Mexico and merges in a clockwise
fashion with the warmer waters of the North Equatorial Current heading straight west to Asia. Parallel with the equator, eventually the current
runs into the northbound Kuroshio current, continuing in a clockwise
manner carrying warm water up north to Japan before the North Pacific

Current completes the massive cyclical transfer of cool and then heated water back to the northern end of the West Coast. So, conversely, a sailor departing Hawaii for California would not take a direct northeast bearing back to the mainland; the typical course would dictate heading up to more northern latitudes before utilizing the prevailing conditions to turn and head back east.

What happens in the center of this broad circular gyre of North Pacific Currents? To someone hoping to cover distance across it, not a whole lot. The middle, or so-called Pacific High, is a proverbial desert—a no-man's-land of high pressure, hot air, and scant wind. The best that you can hope to do is skirt the high.

"The main thing is you have to go south and around the corner of Pacific High," said David Burch, who wrote the book *Celestial Navigation* as well as *The Fundamentals of Kayak Navigation* and *Hawaii by Sextant*. In the mid-'80s Burch was an avid sea kayaker and close personal friend of John Dowd, the Ecomarine shop owner, expedition savant, and editor/founder of *Sea Kayaker* magazine, who was then in close correspondence with Gillet and Kampe in an early business partnership with their kayak shop. Burch, also the director of Seattle's Starpath School of Navigation, had just sailed to Hawaii a few years prior using celestial navigation and had gotten wind of the Hawaii expedition from Dowd.

"It was my recommendation to John to tell whoever was doing this that they were better off starting as far north as they can," Burch said. If he were leaving from San Diego, Burch wanted to impress on this unknown kayaker, it could take months to get anywhere. "The probability of getting some wind (in order to get pushed south), is much higher the more north that you are," Burch said, noting the target of getting "off the bottom corner of the high, where there's some wind circulation."

Gillet certainly understood the larger currents and wind patterns at play as well, establishing a route south to a sweet spot where that noted wind circulation, and the prevailing ocean currents, typically shift clockwise from moving south to west. He knew that starting from San Diego would lower the probability, as Burch mentioned, of immediately catching the winds to shuttle him south. But he also knew that a more southern launch would add the risk of eventually then reaching the trade winds at a point in the ocean much farther east of that sweet spot, thus adding more distance, and more days, to the trip. Plus, leaving from San Diego would likely keep him tracking farther south overall, meaning closer to the summer storm track than he felt was safe. So, he opted to head up the coast, with his sights on Monterey, California, for the launch, an additional 240 miles west and 280 miles north.

The launch location would extend him out more immediately into California Current. A byproduct of the current's cold rush down the West Coast, which provides the shore-bound masses with mild, cool summers characterized by foggy marine layers, is an intense subsurface upwelling. The dynamic in the ocean depths stirs up rich nutrients and oxygenates the water, boosting plankton growth. This foundation of the marine food chain makes the waters off the California coast among the most biologically productive on the planet. For Gillet, it simply meant an immediate increased likelihood of encounters with large marine life. Not that animal migrations were much of a concern when it came to timing.

All Gillet was focused on was his own movement along the ocean surface. He honed in on his optimal time window: leaving in late June to capitalize on the most reliable trade winds in July and August. "Even if it took me until late August to reach Hawaii," he figured, "I would still be off the water before the tropical storm track wandered north of the 20-degree-north parallel as it is likely to do in September."

Sometimes penciled estimates don't always pan out. Gillet got a first whiff of altered speed variables with the first sea trial of the Tofino. On a seventeen-mile transit from San Diego Bay south to the Coronado Islands, a collection of uninhabited crags roughly even with the Mexican border, Gillet budgeted eight hours kayaking there and back alongside a friend. He and Katie, together paddling the Tofino, took all of fifteen hours. He needed to plan for more time at sea.

Otherwise, little had changed in Gillet's approach to launching an expedition as he and Katie loaded the Tofino on the van for the late June drive up to Monterey. Just like on the Sea of Cortez trip with Jardine, Gillet was still tinkering with his setup on the way. This time instead of toe straps, he and Katie were finishing sewing the nylon harnesses that would hold dual inflatable pontoons. Gillet had learned a hard lesson trying to sleep in his kayak on the Pacific Baja trip with Landick, and the pontoons would hopefully constitute a stabilizing system for Gillet to affix to his hull while the kayak stopped. "Improvisation and spontaneity suited my style better than meticulous planning," he said.

Still, the rubber had yet to hit the harness. Arriving in the calm harbor in Monterey, the system seemed to work. The one-time "thought exercise" came to life as Gillet slid the two duffle-size rubber tubes—a pair of thwart cross-sections from a whitewater raft—into the webbing harnesses and inflated them with a bellows-style foot pump he pressed together accordion-style. Perfect fit. It was a little wet and tricky for Gillet to lean forward onto the deck to run the line underneath the hull in order to tie both harnessed pontoons together. But once all tied down, the pontoons snugly cradled both sides of the kayak in its midpoint between the two cockpits. Though he had yet to actually spend a night sleeping inside the kayak, the stabilization system worked and the setup felt solid. Gillet could even stand up as the kayak barely bobbed in the glassy water.

The pontoons were not the only new gear system that Gillet had never used on a prior paddling or sailing trip. The other three new variables to account for were a transmitting system, as well as his big borrow—the Seagold reverse-osmosis water purifier—and, of course, his fiberglass front cockpit hood, customized for internal protection from the elements, maybe even some sleep.

The transmitter was a loaner from Russ Davis, a fellow San Diego sea kayaker friend working as a research oceanographer and teaching at the Scripps Institution of Oceanography. Davis had access to transmitters used to track oceanographic buoys. Every few hours, two French polar-orbiting Argos satellites could sense an electronic Doppler shift in the transmitters, sending both location and temperature data back down to a ground-station computer that was then exported to Scripps, where Davis's lab could monitor the various transmitter locations along ocean currents. Outside of Scripps, no one needed to know that one of those data points was the yellow Tofino lurching slowly southwest to Hawaii.

Davis went one step further, working with research techs at Scripps to disable the stray Argos unit's temperature data transmitter, bypassing it with a rigged jumper wire. The jiggered outbound feed with no temperature data (meaning only location information being sent) was to be interpreted by those monitoring as normal. In other words: No news is good news. Were Gillet to cut the external wire, however, the unit would start correctly transmitting temperature data as well. This conscious act to switch on the data signal would simply mean "watch me closely"—the same kind of heads-up shorthand that Gillet had used while leading rock climbs, shouting down to his belayer before a crux move. In other words: Be prepared, I may fall here. A further disruption in the Argos unit's data transmission, combined with the activation of a separate Emergency Position Indicating Radio Beacon (EPIRB) sailing unit, would mean "Emergency distress. Rescue needed ASAP."

Gillet was still skeptical of the Argos. He'd learned too many times that no matter how meticulous he could be with electronics, vigilantly keeping connections and batteries dry, a sea kayak is just too harsh an environment: "Every electronic device crapped out sooner or later." In an actual emergency, say, "fifty miles from Hawaii and in the water after colliding with a submarine," Gillet liked his chances better with his small EPIRB, which stays off unless needed in an emergency, leaving no one back home to watch and worry. He preferred to travel under that "'no news is good news' principle," less reliant on electronics, even though he had no illusions of even the EPIRB being of any help to him mid-Pacific.

Still, after calling in so many favors, most especially with Katie, he knew he would be on too many emotional radars needing the reassurance of his safety. So, he grudgingly stuffed the bulky aluminum-housed transmitter, antenna, and ninety-day battery into an international-orange PVC tube. Plus, Davis had never seen one malfunction. As the first piece of equipment he loaded into the Tofino, Gillet slid the ten-pound tube to the very nose of the bow and didn't give it another thought.

At the other end of the kayak, Gillet affixed a three-foot tube filled with aluminum foil. This erect tail would constitute a radar reflector that would hopefully be high enough off the water for a passing ship, or perhaps a helicopter, to bounce a signal off of. For good measure, Gillet duct-taped a blinking white man-overboard strobe to the top of the tube and stuck a couple of double-A batteries in it and his self-installed knot-meter.

With the one-way outbound communications systems complete, it was time to focus on the navigation gear as Ed and Katie headed from the harbor back to Monterey Bay Kayaks where he was staging the load. There was no map for this journey across twenty-two hundred miles to Hawaii. A long-range marine single sideband (SSB) radio could, in theory, allow Gillet to call Scripps for the Argos's satellite position, but that expensive an option would also require engineering of a sophisticated, custom electronic system able to charge and store enough power to run it. Commercial handheld GPS units were still two years away, and handheld satellite phones another eleven.

So there in the gear pile was a simple dry box housing all Gillet had available to navigate: a cheap Davis Instruments Mark 25 plastic sextant, an even cheaper plastic backup, as well as a Tamaya NC 77 navigation calculator, plus five waterproof quartz watches and a Radio Shack weather radio. The watches would help fix longitude, synchronized with the weather radio's WWV's shortwave-transmitted time signals. Gillet would be navigating manually, the old-fashioned way. That is, measuring and gauging celestial bodies, then applying rote spherical trigonometry calculations to determine the latitude and longitude of his position.

This was a largely analog venture, with one exception. The calculator's hardwired data replaced an almanac and volumes of navigation tables. With a fixed position input, its ability to calculate distance to a destination—spitting out green fluorescent results onto a one-line, ten-digit screen—replaced the need for a table and plotting sheets (along with the parallel rulers and dividers to determine lines of position and plot a course accordingly). Gillet still packed all the tools and all that text in a bag as well, in case the calculator failed. They weren't the only books he packed. He also brought a modern poetry anthology, a copy of Homer's *Odyssey* ("I have an affinity for epics," he explained), and an empty pocket-size navigation log.

The pile on the outfitter's deck was growing quickly. Gillet had to start fielding a barrage of questions from onlookers and customers who found his motives suspect: Are you trying to kill yourself, or make the *Guinness Book of World Records*? Gillet's enthusiasm drained with each bit of speculation or doubt as "they projected their own fears and insecurities on my trip," he said. "The hardships frightened them: What about the loneliness, the sharks, the waves, storms, the cramped quarters? The rewards were too subtle: Why, why, why?"

To add to the packing distractions, Katie's parents, Peg and Col. Ray Kampe, came down to see Ed off. Gillet felt some pressure as the two Kampes eyed the piles. As veteran sailors, they had packed out extended ocean cruises and even sailed the Singlehanded TransPacific Yacht Race from San Francisco to Kauai. But Ray eagerly helped Gillet test his reverse-osmosis fresh watermaker, successfully cycling five gallons of seawater through it, stabilizing the membrane, and preparing it along with a smaller, Survivor 06 two-pound emergency backup unit. Still Gillet felt the critical evaluation of the retired colonel. He had to know what he thought.

"You did a good job with the kayak. I think you'll make it," Kampe said to a relieved Gillet.

"I was grateful for his positive assessment," Gillet recalled. "I knew that he would call the Coast Guard and ask them to invoke their right to 'terminate a manifestly unsafe voyage' if he didn't believe my kayak was seaworthy. . . . He was one of the few people who thought my trip was not a self-delusional disaster."

Katie's mom, Peg, had another assessment after eyeing the 150-pound pile of canned, foil-bagged, and freeze-dried meals, granola, fruit, ground coffee, powdered milk, and sugar.

"I don't think you have enough food," she said.

Ed and Katie made one final run to the nearby Von's for another bag of food, but Gillet was restless. He had seen it too often at his shop as adventurers provisioned trips into the unknowns of Baja, over-packing "as a way of compensating for feelings of anxiety before a big trip." More so, he was appalled at the extra weight. He needed to cut loose his "mental mooring lines."

Awake at dawn the next day for the launch, Thursday, June 25, Katie insisted on stopping to pick up a few extra bagels on the way into the harbor.

The massive gear load began disappearing into the kayak—the watermakers, the clothes, the food, the endless propane fuel canisters, and the customized medical kit that Gillet's Bay Area ophthalmologist friend, Dr. Creig Hoyt, had designed—all crammed into internal crevices of the eighty-pound fiberglass shell until the seam between the deck and the hull was underwater.

Gillet joked that he would have to eat his way into the kayak, having to secure an extra bunch of unripe bananas next to the spare paddles under the deck bungees.

Adjusting for personal space around an additional bag of apples in the rear cockpit, Katie handed Ed the bagels from the dock. Grabbing a handful of the flavored, most fragrant onions and garlics, he handed the bag back with a dozen plains.

"I have enough food," he told her. "You should keep these for lunch."

Gillet was worried about all the other unknowns. He shivered in the dawn light. He was relieved that this was a low-profile launch—not only to avoid detection from the Coast Guard, who might curtail his launch, but also from the added pressure of fanfare and media attention that would have been involved with sponsor support, "hyping my feat for commercial gain." On the conflicted flip side, however, Gillet also recognized that, had he invested "a deep-pocket sponsor's money to build a highly specialized kayak," the trip might have seemed much saner or safer. Kampe could sense the obvious jitters and handed him his life jacket.

"I don't have any place for this," he told her, handing it back, before compromising and wrapping it around the radar reflector so he could get to the business of paddling the loaded kayak.

After maneuvering it out of the slip, Gillet soon discovered there was zero glide between strokes, like "driving a car with the emergency brake on." He still felt confident in how it handled as he waited for the other two tandem kayaks in his send-off party to join him: Kampe and Dale McCauley, a fellow paddling friend, in another Tofino; and Jeff Schrock, the owner/founder of Monterey Bay Kayaks, and Bob Burroughs, another San Diego photographer friend, in another.

Gillet strained to keep up with the faster double kayaks, aware of how odd he must look to the fishing vessels leaving port, paddling an overloaded kayak from the rear cockpit, deck covered in lines and gear, the front cockpit covered with the domed lid, like "R2-D2 was my paddling partner." Gillet still had yet to test out that final new system at sea: sleeping underneath that hood resembling a robot wingman.

Exiting the harbor into the overcast, cool morning, the pod of three kayaks headed to the one-mile buoy in gently rolling west swell. McCauley tried to humor Kampe, pointing out signs of sea life, but she wasn't having it, muffling an apology as she felt the gravity of the looming departure. Gillet tried to break the tension by asking the other paddlers if they were going to Hawaii too. He went through hugging good-byes to his friends across their kayak seats, ending with Katie.

"I felt stupid and selfish and wanted to call the whole thing off," Gillet recalled, as the two began crying.

Gillet reassured her that he would take the trip one day at a time. "If things aren't right I'll call you from Santa Barbara," he said. "Or I'll land in the Channel Islands and take the ferry home."

"All right, Mr. Ed," Katie said. "Just come home to me, OK?"

Gillet promised, turned, and paddled for the horizon.

CHAPTER FIVE

Into the Gray

Coordinates Unknown
Pacific Ocean
July 2, 1987—Day 8

In the morning darkness, nothing is still. Gillet's loaded twenty-foot boat pitches up and over rolling sets of fifteen-foot swell. The small pair of inflatable pontoons are doing their job stabilizing what now feels far too slender and minimal a craft.

He hasn't seen a vessel or aircraft in days. Nothing close to human contact.

Maybe there's some voice out there, some sign of life. For the sake of reassurance as much as amusement, he pulls out his VHF radio. He turns it to channel 16, the international hailing frequency, and calls out to any possible passing ships in the area. Nothing. *What if I actually needed help?* The questions of rescue contingencies in these empty waters start nagging. He pulls out one of his pencil signal flares for a test, unscrewing the lid and pulling the flimsy chain. POP. *About as loud as a champagne cork,* he thinks as the tiny red phosphorous element hisses up from his hand for two seconds before the wind bats it into the back of a cresting wave. *Useless, even for a roadside car wreck.*

Trying to not think about the hundred-plus miles that now separate him from the nearest road, Gillet downs another thermos lid of coffee. *Time to move.* He pulls in the three-strand line out to the sea anchors, popping off the fiberglass hood fixed over the front cockpit in order to stow the lines and anchors underneath. Though Gillet had intended to use this small dome to cover his own cockpit at night, it didn't take him long to abandon the system. On his first night with the rudimentary hood sealed over him, tied down from the inside, he felt entombed. There was no way to quickly unseal the claustrophobic watertight lid in the event of a flip; water pressure would lock him in the boat. He'd rather take his chances dealing incessantly all night with a spare tarp.

Before deflating the outriggers and stowing them, he prepares for the day ahead: first, filling a water bottle from the tank; stashing a drybag with food for the next few meals in the cockpit; unclipping his bibs to kneel and pee over the side; and, taking advantage of the access, rubbing an emollient combination of a Borofax ointment and hydrocortisone cream on festering sores in his armpits, plus the new ones forming around his waist. As soon as he slides into the torso tunnel of his neoprene spraydeck, pulling it over all of his foul-weather layers, he can immediately feel his damp base layers rub into these new sores. Finally, he removes that bulky life jacket—the one he's only been using as a pillow—from his seat and clips it to the radar reflector pole on the back deck. In place of the jacket, he tosses an orange nylon offshore safety harness over his head, anchoring its line through a steel padeye bolted on the deck. This boat is his floatation device and staying attached to it is all that matters. He adjusts the foam wheelchair pad on his plastic seat, frees his paddle from the deck and then grabs the stretchy outer rand of his spraydeck, reaches forward, and folds it down over the cockpit edge.

The first stroke's dip of blade to water does next to nothing. Gillet settles into the seat, scratching into the sores on his sit bones. He arches his back, straightens his arms and begins rotating his torso, repeating a series of light, short strokes into his custom carbon paddle just to get his full six hundred-pound load moving into the incessant northwest headwind. He needs this baseline momentum. The second that the strokes stop, the boat's forward progress grinds to an immediate halt.

The heavy cloud cover and the constant wind don't just stifle morale and slow progress. No sun means no sense of location. With no dawn or dusk sun sightings to fix his exact position west, celestial navigation is out of the question. The best Gillet can manage is to log distance covered, estimating by dead reckoning. And that's based off a flatwater speed estimate of less than two knots an hour, guesswork based off timed intervals, as the custom spinner-powered electronic knot-meter failed almost immediately.

Not that knowing position really matters. As he drifts south, Gillet is operating by one simple directive: get offshore. The faster he can keep getting west, the better. The goal is to claw out of that ever turbulent and hazardous lane off the California coast that sailors often refer to as "the potato patch," where the current and wind running down and toward the coast conspire to lock travelers onshore. The sooner he can break free of that orbit, at least two hundred miles out, the sooner that he'll have a chance of dealing with calmer seas and, hopefully, catching the return of friendlier trade winds at his back, shuttling him to the islands. *Just get west. Point it right into the wind.*

Every hour of paddling into the gray, set on a compass heading of 210 degrees southwest, Gillet relaxes his strokes. The wind pushes him south, closer to 180 degrees, straight south. He pulls his hood over his face for a moment of respite with the wind at his quarter and revels in the drier, calmer paddling. *Too far south. I'm not going to Catalina Island,* he reminds himself and turns back west, starting to repeat a mantra: "30-130."

That is, 30 degrees north latitude, 130 degrees west longitude, some six hundred miles offshore. It's an arbitrary point in the middle of the ocean. But to Gillet, there couldn't be a destination with more meaning. Until that point—that sweet spot on the corner of the Pacific High—the twenty-plus-knot winds will likely continue. All Gillet can do is counter. Stroke after stroke. He knows he's burning calories; too many. He's working through the final prelaunch food stocks purchased in Monterey much faster than he'd imagined.

However, he is OK with the physical exertion. In his six years of extended sea kayaking expeditions, often solo, he's learned to find comfort in his discomfort, the will to keep moving. Reliance utterly upon himself. Gillet now knows this kayak. The extra reinforced forward volume feels solid handling these conditions. He punches the rockered, bulbous bow through the top of a cresting wave and then slides down the back, momentarily exhilarated. He forgets the bleak surroundings and hones in on the boat running up and down the waves. Bracing through side-swell. *Progress.* Digging through the crests and easing in the troughs, his weighted kayak plows through the heaving fifteen-foot seas. He even catches himself singing as the strokes and hours pass. The exhilaration of powering through the endlessly rolling terrain makes him self-aware that he must be breaking new ground here.

Still no sun or a horizon line. He can only focus on the boat running up and down crashing waves. Side-swell wretches him back into the present. He reaches to brace and cranks on his rudder pedal to swing him farther south, with the prevailing direction of the wind and waves for a few breaths, before cranking the right rudder pedal and turning west toward his target. He can't even imagine the islands. As the rain pounds, all he can see is a compass heading while holding out hope for drier latitudes.

Digging through crests and easing in troughs. The strokes begin to slow. The fleeting distraction of rote paddling is replaced by the return of anxious nags, with each stroke reminding him of the inflamed, festering rashes on the backs of his freckled hands. Thankfully, they are starting to respond to the antibiotics Dr. Hoyt had packed. At the ends of some his strokes, as his hands pass within six inches of his face, he can feel heat radiating off the infection. The monochromatic canvas begins to fade as visibility diminishes to a hundred yards. Gillet keeps plugging away to the point of exhaustion. Except there's no relaxing when he finally stops.

It's a dash to set the anchors before it gets too dark. He pulls off the front cockpit cover and deploys the anchors. Waves are setting up much like the night before, in the ten- to fifteen-foot range. Gillet sets the first anchor out to 150 feet to grab the tops of the approaching swells and shortens the second to around seventy-five feet, accounting for a shorter period, in hopes that it will hold the kayak simultaneously in the waves' troughs. It works. The boat swings into the wind and catches on the waves, tugging the kayak's drift back east to minimize losing all the hard-earned ground covered.

With the boat pointed into the weather, the risk of a boat flip is reduced. Gillet stashes the paddle and grabs one of the limp rubber pontoon tubes and slides it into its webbing harness. He untwists the valve, presses in the pump hose and begins clapping the plastic bellows together. The choppy conditions add to the challenge. He's five minutes in. Starting to drift faster. Without his paddle, Gillet can only react to waves and wind trying to roll the boat: With knees braced under the deck, he absorbs the movements through loose hips and constant counterweight adjustments with his torso. Fortunately, his load of food, gear and a central reservoir of water provides enough ballast for a degree of stability, allowing him to keep jerking air feverishly into the open valve of the first, left tube. Next, he ties the other empty right-side harness to a messenger line on one end of his paddle. Gillet then lances the tied-up blade underwater, leaning forward to slide it beneath the left side of the hull until it pops up on the right, where he pulls up the tangled pile. Now ten minutes into the task, he detaches the harness from the paddle, slides in the second pontoon, finishes inflation duties, and then cinches down the entire assembly to a pair of deck cleats. The routine is at least starting to feel a little more manageable.

No hope for a sundown sighting, Gillet tries to guess his mileage. In flatwater he can paddle the unloaded Tofino as fast as two knots (or 2.3 miles) per hour. Given the headwinds and swell, at ten hours of paddling, and factoring his drift with the swell south, he's likely only logged twenty miles today.

He needs a daily average of more than double that distance if he hopes to reach Hilo, the nearest point in the Hawaiian Island chain, in a projected forty days. He can't think about that distance now. Only 30-130. 30-130.

Heating up a dehydrated meal does little to slow his dejected thoughts: casting huge doubts on his food packing, his overly optimistic timeline. The rain continues, keeping Ed from pulling out his shortwave radio.

The impossible forward progress has halted and he's back to an existence more akin to his multiday climbing expeditions—stuck on the port-a-ledge between pitches on a big wall. Except now he's bivouacked alone. He pulls out his damp sleeping bag and worms inside. The sores on his side sting. Armpits itch. Almost through the hydrocortisone already, he skips his nightly application, knowing he must ration. The waves are increasing. The boat slides down the back of some of the waves, wrenching violently on the anchor line. Without the fiberglass hood, Gillet relies on the pontoons' deck-harness system to also hold down the front edge of a folded tarp that covers the rear cockpit opening. Barely. With loose sides, the tarp whaps in gusting northwest wind.

Mummified in a damp synthetic sleeping bag, Gillet wedges inside the six-foot cavity. His mind is still moving in an exhausted daze of half sleep. He goes through the same vivid fantasy that he's constructed and refined over the last few nights: walking into the marine store in Ventura, California's Channel Islands Harbor, at least a hundred miles to the east. He picks out the same boring beige canvas sheet, then with lucid control of the dreamlike vision, directs his sunny shore-bound self through the steps of fitting and attaching it on an aluminum-tubing frame to his kayak's stern deck. In the final frame, he watches himself pulling the finished bimini-like canopy over his exposed rear cockpit.

But instead of a drier night inside any real version of this imagined dodger, he is already dealing with contingency plans—a backup tarp to keep him from succumbing to total hypothermia. Even somewhat restful sleep, maybe just one ninety-minute REM cycle would help him to recover and to prepare for another consecutive day of marathon levels of exertion.

Focusing back into the vision of the dodger system that could've been, he imagines the canvas hood zippering snugly shut. Closed off from the elements, he would cozily pull off wet outer layers, nestling into a dry sleeping bag and falling into steady sleep with warm dreams of the pig-roast luau celebrating his arrival on the islands.

Suddenly his bow jerks up. It shifts him back in the confined space, head sliding an inch into the rear bulkhead. He's back in the cold, wet sleepless darkness of his living nightmare. As the anchor line stretches, the kayak yaws behind it, lurching the stern right. A wave breaks over the starboard edge. Water rushes over the improvised cockpit cover. Icy buckets pour under and onto the tarp as it sinks onto Gillet's right shoulder. Without opening his eyes or leaving his marine-shop vision, he elbows up the heavy pool to drain. The breach raises saltwater levels inside the coffin-like sleeping quarters just above the plywood sole that keeps Gillet an inch above the hull floor. The water seeps through his bag. The shivering is too much.

Gillet pushes off the drinking-water reservoir at his feet and wiggles up the plastic seat, pulling out an arm to push against the tarp. The wind presses it against him as he emerges from the soaked cocoon. Clouds mask any possible moon or starlight. In the pitch black, he's still wearing everything that he paddled in that day: synthetic Capilene underwear and balaclava hood, polypropylene long-john base layers, dark blue fleece-pile pants and jacket, plus waterproof bib overalls and a hooded raincoat. Nothing is dry. Grabbing the lashed-in handheld bilge pump helps to bail out the water. Each slow jerk on the T-grip handle pulls up and spits out a few ounces at a time. The shivering stops momentarily.

It's still too dark. *Must sleep before tomorrow's haul.* The arm-lurching motion has given Gillet a chance to readjust body position. Once his torso fills the twelve vertical and thirty-one horizontal available inches under deck, he cannot turn over. With shoulders spanning nineteen inches across, the only way for Gillet to adjust on the hard surface, and to keep blood moving, is to undo everything, inch out of the cockpit, roll over, then stuff himself in once again. This time he tries moving his right leg under the compass, which hangs down an additional couple of inches below the deck, and shimmies halfway down into the cockpit and back into his sleeping bag. As he slides onto his left side, he grimaces as the plastic seat rubs the now burning saltwater sores along his butt and legs. He settles in again: adjusts his life-jacket pillow to prop up his head; and then stretches the tarp back down to protect him from the wind and light rain. *No, this isn't purgatory,* he thinks. *This is a sailor's hell.*

He passes out from the shock.

———

The kayak seesaws violently off the back of a wave. Just as he closes his eyes, the dawn's first light pierces through the cover. *Like a knife stabbing me in the face.* He can't remember a shittier night's sleep, though his body's attempts to recover from shock, through cycles of passing out, could barely be called sleep. *Interminable.* Surrendering efforts to rest against the eternal pounding of the elements, he pokes his head out of the tarp to what looks like the exact location he had roused on the day before. Gillet groans, then takes stock: headache, difficulty opening bloodshot eyes, back muscles wretched, fingers slightly pruned, cheeks chapped and windburned. *No use trying to prolong this. Need to stop drifting and keep moving. Coffee first. Need coffee.*

Gillet emerges fully, slowly flips onto his knees. His back aches, fingers dull and numb as he tries to unclip the blue drybag lashed down to his stern hatch cover. He digs out a propane backpacking stove and pan, sets it in the cockpit as he yanks out the damp sleeping bag. Too wet and blustery to hang-dry, Gillet stuffs it down into the roll-top drybag and then hunkers back into the seat. First, he uses the tarp to shield the bitter, cold wind and to light the single burner that screws onto a compressed gas cartridge. Then, with a consistent flame, he carefully lowers the stove's cartridge base between his legs onto the soggy plywood floor. The small pot of water atop the burner lodges just under the cockpit combing, which braces the basic cooking setup through the rolling waves—just enough to keep the soon-boiling water from spilling over onto his legs and crotch.

This time, the alchemy transforming hot water, instant coffee, powdered milk, and sugar into an immediate morale boost doesn't work. Gillet holds onto his warm thermos, scanning the setting. Fog and flat light. No chance at even locating a horizon to take an accurate sun sight means no need to dig out the sextant. No way to calculate longitude and fix his position. He stares down a misty tunnel as low clouds close in around him. *No birds, no dolphins, no fish. Not even a single stalk of kelp to break the monotony of this vast gray wasteland, empty and desolate.* It's at least drier. Enough so that Gillet pulls out the journal he planned to log his positions in. He puts pencil to page for a first entry:

"Day 9: Today, I ate the last of my fresh fruit."

Not much else to say. Eating his last banana still is not enough. He grabs the final onion bagel from that departure-day Monterey pit stop. As he stars blankly at the layer of clouds melding into the horizon, he chews through the dough, snickering at a memory: loading the boat and only grabbing a handful of the flavored bagels. Then reaching up and handing the full dozen back to Katie on the dock. *What a fool! Better savor this bagel.*

After washing down the bagel and prepping the kayak, sleep system stored, anchors in, pontoons dropped, Gillet settles back into his seat. He reaches his left foot forward to push on one of the clunky rudder pedals. It flops loosely forward. He checks the other. Both steel cable lines are slack. He whips around to the sight of half a rudder flapping side to side in the wind. *Fuck.* An instant pulse of nausea unleashes a panicked groan. Gillet had taken weeks working with a machinist to shape and foil that Lexan thermoplastic upgrade onto an overbuilt stainless-steel rudder bracket.

Unconsciously pulling the inflatable pontoon system back out, he imagines what might have happened. The only issue with this custom rudder system was his inability to pull the blade up enough. Ideally a sea kayak rudder would flip out of the water and lock down onto the back deck. He could only pull this one up to just above the waterline, which seemed sufficient for his resting periods. The waves last night must have been steep enough to dip it under. With the anchors lining him up to face swell head-on, he was sliding back down incoming wave faces stern first. Because the anchor lines stretched, they allowed for a few feet of free-planing surf down those waves, enough for the rudder to nosedive into the trough of a wave with nearly six hundred pounds behind it. The force of one of those lunges lined up against the rudder would've been enough.

This is the problem with prototype systems. First-generation concepts must first be tested. Gillet had already learned one lesson with the cockpit cover. This is even more fundamental than suffering through wet, sleepless nights, however. He cannot effectively control or move toward a target, forward or back, without the ability to steer. A crude emergency backup is stowed deep in the back hatch. Gillet goes immediately to work unloading nearly every piece of gear and drybag from the cavernous back section, finding the rudder. He reloads the gear, slips off his layers, and slides his wiry 170-pound frame into his neoprene wet suit, knowing that this installation will not be easy. Or dry.

As he crawls along the back deck, the ever-confused seas compound intensified pulses of nausea. A larger set rolls under the bow and with his bodyweight aft, submerges him chest-deep with the kayak's entire stern section. The cold clamps his lungs shut. He pops up and another wave knocks him off the kayak. Clinging to the kayak's static perimeter line with one hand and the reserve rudder with the other, he notes a couple peripheral stars flashing as he struggles to catch his breath. He vaults up and kicks a leg over the stern, bobbing in and out of the numbing water with his back to the continued ocean chop marching his way.

Up and down, he stares at the rudder bracket amid the constant motion. His stomach turns and he vomits off the side, the last remnants of the final bagel missing his shaking hands. Stomach retched free, Gillet takes a breath and refocuses on the single task ahead. He taps into the same mandatory presence gained through years of climbing, clutching the spare rudder in hand with the same fixed attention needed to set to anchors a thousand feet up when your muscles beg you to rest. He pulls off the Lexan scrap and tosses it into the ocean. *Do not drop the pin,* he tells himself calmly as he slides in the spare, replacing the pin, and giving it one check before returning to his cockpit. He collapses into the seat, catching his breath. *We're OK.*

With a warm cup of cider in his hands, Gillet reassesses his situation. He tries to look at it objectively: Yes, the homemade rudder is big enough to steer the kayak. Yet it is marginal at best, a basic fiberglass-coated shape cut with jigsaw from a sheet of plywood in his garage. This whole idea—trying to crudely paddle an off-the-shelf kayak to Hawaii—is marginal. He's soaked, with no hope of drying out thanks to a poorly conceived cockpit cover. He's burning through more calories and covering less distance per day than he had ever estimated. He's getting pushed too far south. And now there's no spare rudder.

Outmatched and underprepared. Rationally, Gillet thinks how this compromised journey makes no sense. The shakedown provided valuable lessons learned. There are no financial costs, as he bought this production kayak on a commissioned sale for less $2,000. All in, he's only spent $7,000, all of his own and Katie's money. There's also no pressure to finish this trip. He has no sponsor obligations to fulfill. There will be no media inquiries. No letdowns.

And without much other thought, and no outward emotion, he digs into the spare rudder. "Screw this," Gillet says to himself as he sets a course downwind and begins hauling ass. South and east. Back to San Diego. He can be home in another nine days.

CHAPTER SIX

Commitment

San Diego

ON THE MORNING OF JULY 3 BACK IN SAN DIEGO, KATIE KAMPE STARTS her day like every one that she's had since the drive north to launch Ed in Monterey: opening the shop. She fires up the VW bus and heads over to the Southwest Kayaks shop on Rosecrans, the main avenue running through the string of small businesses servicing the San Diego Bay side of the Point Loma peninsula, the extended arm that forms the western boundary of the city's sprawling bay-harbor complex. To differentiate from Point Loma's other marine stores, sportfishing outfitters, and restaurants, Kampe pulls out one of the bright yellow Necky sea kayaks to display on the hedge out front. The shop may not be on the water, but as she likes to say, it's only "a hoot and a holler, couple blocks and left turn to Shelter Island," where customers can launch onto the protected Pacific waters of the bay.

A waterfront location wouldn't have been imaginable financially anyway. "When we started, we had nothing," Kampe recalls of the $400 left in her checking account. Word about the shop, however, is slowly starting to spread. As the city's only kayaking specialty retailer, the daily handful of new-customer walk-ins is slowly increasing by an interested customer or two. With Ed gone, Katie needs help.

"I had to make it work," Kampe says of the new business, "because it was in my name as the sole proprietor."

Fortunately, she draws from a well of determined motivation and a forthright sensibility described by friends like Bob Licht as "pedal to the metal at all times." Still, she can't do it all alone. And new to the area and without many local options, Kampe enlists help from the familiar Sausalito-area Sea Trek circle of paddlers where she used to row. Alex Oppedyk, a sea kayak instructor from the Netherlands, offers to lend a hand. As a close friend willing to change scenes from one California bay to another, Oppedyk's arrival is crucial.

"Thank god for Alex," she says. "He didn't want anything out of it. He was just there to help me and do something different, and he didn't even know Ed."

At thirty-three, the pressure is on Katie with the success of her new business in the front of her mind. Of course, thoughts of Ed are never far. Amid the activity of the first few days getting Alex up to speed on the shop, fielding requests from new customers, and figuring out how to sell the boats offered on consignment terms, each day Kampe gets a call from Russ Davis's lab over at the Scripps Institution of Oceanography. When she hears the position transmitted from the jury-rigged Argos device buried in her husband's kayak bow, she pins it on a chart tacked to the wall.

A few friends of the shop understand the chart. In Kampe's focus on day-to-day business, she hasn't bothered making it expressly known to customers what the map is for, let alone advertise or make efforts to somehow leverage, for the sake of marketing, the otherwise newsworthy journey so intimately connected to the shop. Because of the apparent scale of the trip, those in the know wander in asking for updates. And each day that she adds a new pinpoint, new queries mount from folks in the shop as well as calls from Ed's family.

When she hears today's numbers, she reads them back to double-check. Surprisingly, the pinpoint deviates from the line that she has been marking on the map. Instead of following the path south and just a little west, this location is the opposite direction: east, on a heading for San Diego.

"OK," Kampe recalls thinking analytically, "he's decided it's not going to work and is turning around."

In Ed's kayak, the thinking is not as resolute. The transmitter device has picked up the variation, a result of Gillet's three productive hours spent cruising east, finally covering miles and enjoying the wind at his back. Though after around fifteen miles back toward the coast, he stops to assess the situation. Gillet's rational self, the louder one reassuring him to take the lessons offered and live for another day, begins to quiet.

The conversation begins.

Gillet considers breaking his own best rule. That is, if your instincts tell you to turn around and you listen, never rethink the choice. It's all too easy to second-guess a trip-altering choice once the stress that precipitates it disappears.

On Gillet's South America trip three years earlier, he took an entire day to contemplate a return to his original starting point in Punta Arenas, Chile, to tend to an impacted wisdom tooth. With no partner to clarify ideas, offer perspectives, or perhaps provide affirmation, he was left to cross-examine himself, looking at the situation neutrally to ensure that the choice to retreat was not a function of short-term emotions. Certain that he'd selected the best possible decision given the circumstances with his tooth—to indeed turn back—Gillet reversed three weeks' work and didn't look back. In five days, he erased the ninety hard-won miles spent clawing into fifty-knot headwinds up the Magellan Strait.

This time, the voices doubting retreat cannot be silenced. Especially considering one important what if: "If I return home, will I really ever do this again? Will I fix the boat, spend the money, make the time?"

No. It's too hard, too marginal. There is no way I will generate the momentum, muster the will. There's no way I can leave Katie alone with the shop again. No way. This is it. This is THE shot.

"Am I going to live?" Self-doubt wonders.

If I'm gonna die, I'm gonna die, but whatever. I'm going for it.

With the thought of death, the rational mind speaks up again. Except this time, Gillet can bend the logic a bit. If he decides to return, yes, he'll get back safe, but where will he land? In Mexico somewhere? What a pain in the ass to figure a way home. "So, do I have enough food?" *Well, it looks OK.* Plus, the weather seems to be starting to turn. Gillet even considers the possibility of getting a first sun sight as the clouds begin to reveal patches of blue.

"And what of this pain and unnecessary suffering?"

Those are just short-term, nothing physically significant. The discomfort is just emotional.

"What did you expect?" the objective mind begs. "You're offshore so there's rough weather. You broke a rudder. That's why you brought a spare. You're still reasonably healthy."

"Anything else wrong?"

Nope.

"Well suck it up, you're burning daylight."

So he breaks his rule. This time it's definite. This *is* it. He digs into his reserve rudder once more and turns his back on the coast. He heads directly into the wind once again. A first wave breaks over the deck and splashes him in the face to immediately bring his choice to life.

"I WILL DO THIS," he yells into the elements. *Hawaii or bust!*

No more time for what-ifs, Gillet thinks. *No more brooding wandering thoughts.*

He cannot worry about tomorrow. Only about paddling over the next hundred yards.

Paddle strongly for the next hour. This day will pass.

And as the labored strokes start to add up, backtracking the back-tracked miles, the hours start to pass.

The distant patches of blue widen to fuller splotches. Gillet shifts his focus to follow the movement above. Overhead, the sun is still a hazy disk. A midday sun sighting through his sextant will only help him determine latitude. At "local apparent noon," that is, when the sun is at the highest point of its east-to-west path—and thus to the Northern Hemisphere observer on a direct line of longitude south to the equator—determining degrees of latitude above the equator is a simple calculation derived from the sun's angle at its peak from the horizon. Still, without morning or evening sights to help determine longitude, necessary in order to fix his approximate location, Gillet has no idea how far offshore he has made it. But after nearly two weeks of simply following a compass heading toward a gray horizon, those patches offer much-needed hope, not only for accurate morning sun sights, but also a chance to warm up and dry off.

Feeling better, Gillet decides to document the moment. He digs out his Nikonos camera and holds it out on the end of his paddle blade, turning the lens back to capture this resolved self. With furrowed brow under his neoprene hood, focused on keeping the camera balanced, he squints through the breeze and brighter conditions to look straight into the lens. Face chapped, eyes intent, no smile.

Stroke after stroke, hour after hour, and finally day after day staying in this newly focused space, Gillet's latent voice of objectivity interludes back into his journal. He assesses a string of days constituting, "the worst of my life." More wet and heavy exertion by day and tortured discomfort by night. The periods of rest and weathered paddling blend into one another, dissolving into "a fog of fatigue, pain, bone chilling cold, fear, and misery." The entry's laconic tone captures the desperation: "Felt like dying. Relentless weather. High exposure. Felt like I was in a life raft."

By Day 14, the gray stratus layer lifts. The sight of puffy cumulus clouds boosts spirits. Clearer skies provide a degree of contrast as the water goes from gray to a steelier shade of blue. The wind even shifts to a favorable enough side angle to fly his parafoil kite. Gillet had bought the kite—a multicolored fifteen-square-foot parafoil made from one-ounce ripstop nylon spinnaker cloth—for his 1982 solo from Glacier Bay, Alaska, down the Inside Passage to Seattle. He never had the right fifteen-knot winds to fly it and only mastered hand-launching and using it on the gusting central coast of Chile. The little kite has less impact on his heavier loaded double kayak, but Gillet is grateful for any iota of extra boat speed. This feels like progress slightly west to 30-130.

Are those trees?

The long-awaited sight of a clear horizon seems to be playing tricks on Gillet. He fixes his gaze. With subtle movement, he makes out radio masts in the distance. Ships and helicopters start to appear, a full naval convoy headed toward San Diego.

Gillet's resolve is still there; he shuts down the urge to ask for a ride. There's still something he can gain from the encounter. He grabs his VHF radio but stops to consider proper radio protocol: *What is the name of this vessel?*

Gillet has never named one of his kayaks. As an extension of himself and his own willpower, akin to a bicycle or pair of skis, naming a kayak he's told his sailor friends, "would be superfluous, like naming each of your shoes or gloves."

The convoy is moving fast, about twenty knots, so he rattles off a call to the lead ship a quarter-mile away.

"Eastbound naval vessel about 450 miles west of San Diego, this is . . . the *Dolphin*, over."

"This is the USS *Ramsey*. What vessel is calling? Over."

"I'm the yellow kayak off your port bow and I'm flying a multicolored kite, maybe you can see that. Over."

After a tense wait, where Gillet can only imagine the scene on the bridge—sailors scanning the water with binoculars, wondering if they are being pranked, the *Ramsey* confirms that they see him. However, they decline to offer their course. At Gillet's request, they do at least share their position. That gesture allows Gillet a reference point to check his crude navigation estimates without a single accurate sun fix. The verdict: 32 degrees north, 125 degrees west.

Really? That's only about four hundred miles due west of San Diego, on a line of longitude even with the edge of Washington's Olympic Peninsula, the westernmost point of the contiguous United States. That reading, roughly even with the US-Mexico border, means he's drifting too far south, too close to the storm track crossing the Pacific at 20 degrees north latitude. Before he stews any more on the underwhelming reading, he asks a question to the officer cruising away in the 415-foot frigate: Can he please call his wife, Katie, and relay the message that he is in good shape and heading for the islands?

After reading off her phone number and hearing the ship's confirmation, Gillet feels better. Imagining Katie receiving the news update from the navy softens the blow of his dismal progress. He turns his thoughts to the Argos, with renewed interest in covering miles. He imagines Katie receiving the updates from the invisible signals pulsing out of his bow, her resting easy at his increased mileage on the day.

What he cannot imagine, however, is that something is happening inside the tube holding the Argos unit antenna and battery. Or, more accurately, that something is not happening. Interference with the ship's radar causes the Argos transmitter oscillator to stall. As Gillet paddles away from the USS *Ramsey* encounter, he has no idea, or way of knowing, that there's a problem with his one crude tool for outbound communication home.

Fortunately for Gillet, communication is not, and has never really been, a necessity. Growing up in Miami, he found solace from an early age in the immediate escape of the ocean. Riding bikes with his two younger sisters, Catherine and Mary, from their home in Coral Gables out to Key Biscayne, his fondest childhood memories are rooted in his own individual, independent experience, discovering coral fish in a separate, alternate world.

"I liked free diving and snorkeling because that's another really solo sport," he recalled. "You can't exactly carry on a conversation. You might be with other people but it's much more immersion in a completely different environment."

He dabbled in organized sports, swimming, and a little football, but ultimately veered in his high school years to the more cerebral challenges of chess and the speech and debate clubs. "I didn't need a lot of human connection," says Gillet, who gravitated back toward withdrawn endeavors on his own, especially in the ocean.

"As much as he did very arduous physical things," remembers his sister Catherine, "there was always a philosophical, existential component to it. Without sounding too pretentious, he was definitely an intellectual young person, and I idolized him. He thinks very deeply about whatever he's going to do or what he's going to say or how he comes across and presents himself and what he cares about—he cares deeply about things."

Their father, Ed Gillet Sr., cared about getting his children out on the ocean every weekend opportunity that he could. With freckled, fair skin like her brother, Catherine was not interested, and would go "only if we were forced to." Her brother, however, immediately took to sailing, learning from his father at the tiller of a small Sabre dinghy around the harbor.

When Gillet's parents divorced, his sisters remained with his mother while he moved up to Coconut Grove to live with his father and attend a Jesuit high school. This also meant more time closer to the harbor. When Gillet turned sixteen, Dad didn't buy him a car. Ed Gillet Sr. gave his son a sixteen-foot Luger kit sailboat.

"I would just sail south as far as I could, see how far I could get, if I could get to the keys," Gillet recalls. He'd push farther each trip. One Sunday he got as far as Ellie Key just as the sun was setting. Without enough daylight to return home, he decided to spend the night on board. He used a brick to anchor himself, then lay down in the bottom of the small cabin-less craft.

"I remember listening to the dolphins swimming by at night and I could hear them breathing," he says. "I remember feeling like this was a really cool adventure, but I don't remember being scared."

"That's just the way he is—he's steady Ed," Catherine explains of her brother's Zen-like even keel. "He doesn't get too crazy about anything—one foot in front of the other and gets the job done: what he sets his mind to."

The focus brought Gillet the fifteen-some miles back early the next Monday morning, just in time for his high school classes, where he felt a deep sense of accomplishment. After college in Florida, that acute need to keep pushing himself physically and intellectually moved him to the West Coast with his first wife. He found the perfect fit in a philosophy PhD program at the University of California, San Diego, with challenging course work on a campus looming dramatically over the Pacific. The marriage, however, was not a perfect fit. When the relationship went south, so did Gillet. He left academia for the ocean, to run sailboat charters out of Acapulco, where he delivered yachts up and down the Pacific Coast. As delivery ranges stretched, he started to get a feel for the desolate realities in the middle of the ocean, finally running a two-mast clipper-like CT-41 ketch from Lahaina, Maui, to San Diego in thirty-six days.

Gillet remained close with his father, routing his kayak trip to South America through Miami, and returning there, catching up with him as he processed the journey and wrote up the experience in a series of commissioned articles. Gillet Sr. enjoyed tracking his son's exploits, proud to keep family and friends informed of the accomplishments. The voyage alone to Hawaii, however, seemed different—"too hairball, naked, and dangerous to be sane," Gillet projected of his father's wary read on it.

In a position of defense, Gillet reiterated to his father first and to his family that "he wouldn't be doing if he didn't think he could," Catherine recalls. "He said it a bunch of times. Something that he kept expressing was he knew and believed that he could do this."

Gillet's sister trusted his confidence in preparation, "that he made the judgment he would be able to survive it." His father still had his doubts, going as far as reaching out to his son's close friends, including a psychotherapist, in hopes of persuading Gillet to change his mind.

It was no use. Gillet's deep-seated belief in his ability to survive was enough. Enough to launch. Enough to push him on, to continue past the encounter with the USS *Ramsey*. Though he had gained so much open-ocean awareness while sailing years ago on what would be his ultimate kayak route, and now, over the last two weeks, had internalized the realities of offshore exposure in such a visceral and trying way, Gillet must now reckon with a single nagging murmur of doubt. The low-simmering feeling that boiled over with the miserable days was compounded by the emergency-rudder mishap. Even with his new, steadfast resolve to continue west, a little, yet constant, voice still remains grounded in uncertainty. A reminder of his situation at once exhilarating but also calling for alarm. A strange, new normal state of being that needs recognition and that demands respect.

In preparing for this journey, he had tried to anticipate the unknowns, neutralize variables, and assess every problem he would possibly encounter. He planned backups, and contingencies, and thought out emergency responses. But what Gillet feared most was knowing there were factors that he did not know, eventualities he'd not even considered. What he knew was that he was "not likely to die from any of the risks I knew about."

What he did not know about was the same weather phenomenon few climatologists then understood. What he did not factor in was El Niño.

CHAPTER SEVEN

30-130

GILLET FIRST HEARD OF EL NIÑO WHILE PADDLING ALONGSIDE STEVE Landick during the pair's 1982 southbound kayak transit of the Baja Peninsula's Pacific coast. Talking about dream paddling trips to South America, Landick shared the tale of a sailor riding a rare north wind down the Peruvian coast, taking advantage of a cyclical weather anomaly that countered the otherwise prevailing Humboldt Current, responsible for ushering cold water up from the Southern Ocean. It made Gillet wonder about the reversal; he would come to know the northbound current well, paddling with it on his continental voyage up South America's west coast and past Peru.

He didn't think much of this little-known anomaly though, especially one that didn't seem to amount to much more than periodic warming of sea-surface temperatures in the eastern-central equatorial Pacific. There, South American fishermen first noticed the deviation in their nearby waters around Christmastime and thus named El Niño for the Christ child. But by the time Gillet and Landick neared Los Cabos at the end of 1982, finishing off their nine hundred–mile blitz in an impressive thirty days, the far-reaching consequences of a significant El Niño event were made alarmingly real. Atypical south swells often prevented the duo from landing. Unusually high tides and punishing surf closed off suddenly exposed beaches normally protected in the early winter from prevailing weather from the north and west. That left Gillet and Landick extending already long days into nights on the water, pushing fifty to ninety miles between landings.

By the time they made their approach into Cabo San Lucas, a late-season tropical depression wrought a storm with sixty-knot winds that wrecked at least thirty sailboats and stranded yachts in the harbor—the result of a 1982–83 weather event, then the strongest El Niño–Southern Oscillation event ever recorded, and still ranking as the one of the top three to have earned the standard-setting Oceanic Niño Index's "very strong" rating.

Four years later, as Gillet prepared to launch out of Monterey, he had no idea that he was doing so at the tail of a "strong" two-year El Niño cycle. Neither did the experts.

"At the time of his trip, oceanographers had a simplistic view of El Niño, its causes and its prediction," Russ Davis, the Scripps professor of oceanography wrote, noting the experimentation happening with forecasting models. "These had, at best, lead times of two to three months and we now know they are not successful in explaining many of the more recent El Niños. . . . Even the optimists did not then believe that predicting the El Niño that was so important to Ed was possible from data available when he left."

To Gillet, the '82 landing episode with Landick in Cabo was an outlier, and one that wasn't well understood at that. He figured the shifts were more local anyway, likely only affecting those volatile stretches of Peru and northwestern Ecuador where his South America trip ended too soon. Gillet would calculate and budget his Hawaii timeline on statistically based seasonal weather predictions—models gauged on averages that are right 90 percent of the time.

The consequences of an El Niño event, however, are anything but predictable. Altering the climate interaction between the ocean and the atmosphere has large-scale impacts. Normal jet streams shift latitudes, simultaneously creating flood and drought risks. The wide array of irregularities can be linked back to wind patterns that reverse the direction of the eastern-central Pacific so that it flows east, raising the ocean's surface temperatures and, in turn, forcing tropical disturbances and storms to travel farther north than normal.

On the other hand, the North Pacific High—the vast anticyclone of high pressure in the northeastern Pacific between Hawaii and California that slowly circulates air clockwise—can shift farther south toward the equator sooner than normal in the summertime. If the high shifts south, then Gillet's 30-130 target is off. Rather than skirting the high and catching fresh and constant northeasterly trade winds running along its south edge, he may very well be steering a course right through it.

By Day 19 Gillet begins to wonder what is happening with the wind. Perhaps the indications of high pressure with these weaker, intermittent winds are the sign of a broader climatic shift like he experienced five years ago. For three days now, it has been too light to launch his kite. At the very least, it is no longer in his face, shifting ever slightly to the north. As the wind lightens as well, the sky begins to clear and the air warms. He can begin to dry out and better assess his new living accommodations, emerging as if he has just made it through a long, hard winter. Spring cleaning starts with drying out his sleeping bag on the radar reflector tube behind his seat, hoping the UV light can do something to neutralize the mold that spots nearly every inch of nylon. With a much-needed change out of his foul-weather gear and into dry layers, the milder conditions immediately provide relief for his saltwater sores. To heal the sores, each needs multiple daily applications of hydrocortisone cream and Borofax ointment. It becomes immediately clear that there is not enough packed of either. This shortage constitutes Gillet's first item rationed. From now on, just enough cream to control the sores from getting worse.

After redistributing rummaged food bags to provide the right ballast, Gillet assesses his lot. He's still got a decent reserve of water at fifteen gallons. The only other equipment failures are his shortwave radio and the internal lighter for his propane stove—a problem made worse after he discovers a leak in the box housing his spare lighters. He adds the soaked waterproof matches to the chore list of items needing to be dried out. He even dismantles the radio circuit board to give it a rinse in fresh water. The de-salt and dry-off does the trick. Soon Gillet is paddling with a hot cup of coffee and listening to NPR's *All Things Considered*, adding up to "a day of small victories." Nights still pass in pain and great discomfort, but drier conditions mean hours of actual sleep. Bouts of sunshine improve Gillet's immediate mood; he's even singing songs to pass the time. The big picture, however, isn't as cheery.

By Gillet's calculations, he's been drifting about ten miles a day for the last week, and propelling himself an additional twenty-five miles per day. Now, twenty days in, he can close in on his 30-130 target (30 degrees north, 130 degrees west) at this pace in the next few days. But 560 miles into the voyage, that's only a quarter of the total distance to Kona, Hawaii. At thirty-five miles a day, he'll need another fifty days! He knows he has nowhere near enough food to subsist for that long.

With such a long horizon, all Gillet can do is narrow to the now. Focus on the day. "I pinned my hopes on the 30-130 point as the place where my luck would change." He goes through the motions, attentively finishing his day and preparing the kayak for rest: set a long and a short sea anchor; watch the bow swing into the light wind; pump up the outrigger tubes; fit them into the webbing cradles, cinch them down, and secure the backup rudder in place; enjoy a dinner favorite of freeze-dried beef Stroganoff; chocolate bar and ibuprofen for dessert; finished by a cup of hot Tang and then a cup of strong tea with lots of milk and sugar for good measure. After dark, the horizons shrink further to "the limits of the weak circle of light cast by my headlamp." Within that immediate radius, Gillet assesses his surroundings. He begins to get a feel for the spot that he is bedding down for the night. The sights, the smells, the clouds above and the depths below: He's beginning to understand the unspoken labels of a unique place—like a distinct campsite he might recognize were he to ever return. The day ends with a degree of contentment in the limited scope of his personal bivouac at sea.

Though the calm conditions allow him to rest, Gillet's anxiety returns upon waking in the flats. Having calculated the dire amount of distance remaining, he takes a closer look at his food stocks only to discover that he has eaten through half of his inventory, despite covering just over a quarter of the total miles. In other words, what remains stretches out to about twenty more days of food, tops. He tries to break down the distance with some optimistic math: If the wind stays favorable, blows at least, say, fifteen to twenty knots, hopefully picking up a little more trade-wind-driven base current, and he can paddle and sail for thirteen hours a day, that will get him to around seventy-five miles a day. At that clip, he can reach Hawaii in another twenty days.

If the wind will blow. *This is the problem with inductive reasoning*, Gillet considers, *assuming the future will be like the past.* He imagines those seductive blue wind arrows on his pilot chart that simply represent statistical constructs, averages of big year-to-year variances that somehow represent a normal year. Therefore, those lines *must* reflect reality. What's happening off the chart is not normal. *Any day now*, he reassures himself, *I shall be released.*

In the meantime, he decides to make some variances in his routine. He props his butt up onto the rear deck of the kayak and kneels on his life jacket, switching to his bent-shaft canoe paddle to break up the monotony of double-blade repetition through flatwater. Landick and Kruger were huge proponents of using canoe paddles with seafaring kayaks and Gillet begins to understand why. He enjoys switching to different muscles with a higher leverage point, steering the boat with his strokes instead of the foot pedals controlling the rudder. With the action and task at hand, Gillet even feels a strange connection to pan-Pacific Polynesian forebears. He goes with it and belts out a few made-up paddling chants in an imaginary language.

He inhabits that connection to the ocean's ancestral navigators. Thinking back on how he had identified his campsite last night, he looks to the ocean ahead, chanting and paddling, actively working to listen to the more subtle and mercurial characteristics of the water. The Polynesians found their way by interpreting the nearly imperceptible, the slightest rock of the boat or shift in the wind, to determine complex patterns of swells and currents reflecting around distant land masses. Gillet paddles, scanning the water ahead and his senses within, attempting to observe all and to catalog an entirely new place.

At sixteen hours, Gillet arrives at his next "campsite," exhausted, upper body fatigued. His "cabin" still feels like a coffin—feet on the water tank, head on the angled seat. Wet, cramped, sore, and itchy, Gillet tries something new to rest as well. He takes half of one of the Halcion sleeping tablets that Dr. Hoyt prescribed. The .25 milligram of nervous system depressant results in four hours of uninterrupted, restful sleep—the best he's gotten the entire trip.

As he sleeps, the kayak drifts past the now arbitrary marker of 130 degrees west. The self-imposed meridian-line boundary runs up to the edge of the Alaska Panhandle. He's been under the 30-degree north parallel for five days, on the southern border of the "horse latitudes," so-called for the subtropical ribbon of high pressure that becalmed Spanish ships heading to the West Indies, prolonging voyages and stretching supplies that forced sailors to throw depleted livestock overboard. The same high pressure that stifles wind and precipitation locally runs through lands made arid around the globe; Gillet is even with the Sonoran and Chihuahuan Deserts, on a line east through Houston and New Orleans that extends through the northern ends of the Sahara and Arabian Deserts. Like that, 30-130 comes and goes.

When he wakes, the dead calm makes him still feel like a body at rest. Not one set in motion. *This must be some kind of dome of high pressure,* he thinks, though unlike a sailor he cannot just turn on a motor and head to lower latitudes where he might hope to find lower pressure and breezes. He's practically stationary in the middle of the Pacific, completely at the whim of the weather, *like a skydiver locked into a trajectory.*

"Day 26," Gillet begins, penning in his journal. "Another fucking calm day, on westerly light winds. Shitfire do I feel desperate. Barometer climbing so maybe I'm past the trough. Don't know whether to rest dry out, conserve energy, or to do everything I can to paddle out of the hole. According to pilot chart this shouldn't be happening. Got VHF working with a battery pack. Would consider rescue or ride at this point, but no one in the vicinity.

"Feel like I've hung myself and it's going to take another 30 days to die," Gillet sighs with this final thought to close the entry, then looks around, before adding a final note, "At least it's warmer."

To make matters worse, the next day the winds shift more to head on, coming right from the direction, southwest, that he is headed. The most Gillet can do is sit behind sea anchors to slow the drift. He listens to the radio broadcast of Oliver North's congressional testimony on his role in the Iran-Contra scandal. The sound of human voices helps remind Gillet of his remoteness. It sharpens his appreciation by having such removed perspective on the small, distant doings of man from his position alone among such sheer enormity of space. The exposure also reminds him to do another food inventory. He soon decides it's time to start eating half rations—and that he also needs to supplement his diet somehow. He hangs a fishing lure over, but in the crystal clear water cannot even see small fish. He jigs it up and down a few times and then gives up.

He does happen upon some old fishing floats, the flotsam covered in thick clusters of gooseneck barnacles. Gillet gives one a taste and recoils. *Ugh,* hairy and tough. He grabs a few and boils them in a little water, discovering a semi-palatable stew. The caloric concoction becomes a daily meal supplement.

The debris covered in barnacles is one thing. The trash that he experienced earlier, on Day 23 he thinks, was due to something else, perhaps overboard materials in the wake of the Transpac sailing race. The refuse sightings continue into Day 28 when he journals of "crossing a big tide line with floating shoes and Styrofoam trash," right into "soupy water with lots of pulsating jellyfish."

Gillet has no idea how, in ten years, during the next largest record-breaking El Niño on record, Capt. Charles Moore will make a discovery here. It's one that will cast a unique spotlight on this otherwise empty area of the Pacific somewhere between 20 and 40 degrees north latitude. Following the return route from Hawaii to Southern California, after a 1997 Transpac race, Moore decided to take a shortcut home. Rather than follow the traditional sailing route, with the prevailing wind and currents north of Hawaii before heading back east to the mainland, he took a direct, rhumb line straight back. This put him well into the midst of an expanded North Pacific High, where he made startling observations at the top of the water column.

"It wasn't very impressive," says Moore. "Just a piece here, a piece there." And the bits of trash—nothing that would interfere with navigation, simply shards and semi-submersed items with low windage—was far from anything resembling a visible mass or island. But going back through his log, the sparse sightings added up "enough to make me want to come back and measure it."

For the next fifteen years, Moore's subsequent expeditions (through his Algalita Marine Research Foundation) into the desolate middle of the high documented a phenomenon that has gotten "sixty times worse by count and a couple hundred times worse by weight." He coined the label the Pacific Garbage Patch. It describes the massive hundred-million-ton mass of plastic particles swirling together and caught in the middle of the circular currents of the North Pacific Gyre. As Moore and other scientists have established a body of research on the collection of trash, the terminology has been updated to the Eastern or the North Pacific Garbage Patch, also to differentiate it from the ocean's other "garbage patch" collections that amass in other gyres located in the northwest Pacific and southeast Pacific.

All Gillet knows is that what he is paddling through feels like crossing a watery, trashy desert. The sense of life suspended in a gyre resonates.

He journals how the eerie mid-ocean standstill feels "like a curse." That night the calmness takes on a heavier weight. The boat steadies as if sitting on a slab of marble. The inky water below mirrors the hemisphere of starlight above. He stirs the cool water and phosphorescent plankton explodes in every direction. All he can do is revel in a strange disembodied sense of weightlessness, floating somewhere in deep space.

In this dark, disorienting purgatory, the stillness begins to feel like death. He needs to move to survive. Gillet must start paddling out of the void. He generates forward momentum, a path lighting up behind him like a comet's tail in the phosphorescence, so bright off his bow that it makes it difficult to read his 250-degree compass heading. He looks back up to the stars, using Spica, the bright tip of Virgo, to guide him westward. A bit of wind wisps his face to bring him back from the trance. Yet now every thought is driven by a new pressure to move. *Every decision, every stroke, every chore must be performed with an eye on moving west with the utmost efficiency!*

Gillet begins pushing his daily paddling times up to sixteen hours, often feeling stuck on a treadmill, making no progress in relation to the clouds. His Day 31 morning calculation puts him at just over twenty-seven miles a day, with fourteen hundred miles to go . . . meaning still another fifty days to go.

His focus snaps back to food. *How much should I be eating? How much should I be conserving?* "Well, if you run out of food, you can always suffer," the offhand joke from Gillet's friend Milan Zobeck prior to the launch begins to haunt him. *How much suffering can I really take?* Food is never far from his thoughts. He knows he is now losing weight despite gaining muscle. He's slurping down barnacle stew whenever he can to keep him from dipping further into the food stores. There's no fish schooling around the kayak, no mahi hiding in kelp patches, and not enough speed to troll a line. That thirty-first night, despite taking a full Halcion, Gillet wakes from a nightmare. It's the same one: back in Monterey, handing the bag of bagels up to Katie.

The crossing is starting to feel less like an expedition paddling a kayak, and more like an experience adrift in a life raft.

CHAPTER EIGHT

Sink or Swim

July 26–August 21, 1987—Days 32–58

On Day 32, just after his noon sun sighting, fresh trade winds start to blow. Gillet sits upright. His strokes regain purpose. He leans forward, reaching more with each stroke, trying to coax all available speed. Getting the "life raft" up to what he estimates as five knots, the hours melt away as the wind sustains. *Finally*, Gillet thinks as he even catches a wave, *reprieve from a death sentence*. He launches the kite, flying it high for once, well above the windswept troughs and peaks, catching even stronger precious, sustained air blowing from the northeast.

The trades blow through the night. Gillet wakes to the welcome sound of wind whistling through the lines running off the top of his radar reflector. After eight days of calm, punctuated by only fluky zephyrs, and frustratingly contrary headwinds, he revels in a singular sight all around him: *blue, foam-flecked waves surging toward Hawaii*.

"These are the days," Gillet writes in his log, first after a productive morning spent pumping a fresh two and a half gallons of water. Then with a north-northeast wind, and an afternoon of fast paddling that lasts through the evening, he keeps riding the conditions, not swapping the paddle and kite for his outriggers and sea anchors until midnight.

The warm trades continue at fifteen to twenty knots. Gillet grounds in the moment to commit the scene to memory—*joyously frothy water like royal-blue champagne. Warm, clear, sparkling, with highlights of indigo, violet, and electric blue; bolts of sunlight flashing through heaving swells like lightning.* He's free from plodding in purgatory. His stern lifts, and he starts paddling furiously to catch the rolling face of a ten-foot wave. Then he quickly eases off. *Not too much*—he'll kill his speed in the trough, or if he accelerates too much, enter the back of the next wave. *Weave through the hilly water like a skier working moguls.*

Each roll of surf is an extra fifty yards to his goal. Every wave caught is a leap ahead of his standard steps toward the islands. He thinks of Katie, wishing she could see him in action, maneuvering the craft in heavy, favoring seas as he had envisioned. She must be watching this from afar, tracking this significant uptick in distance made. The day blurs by in hundreds of caught waves, Gillet trailing a fishing line in water he imagines must be home to mahi.

A squall line appears behind him. The wall of dark clouds builds and passes over. The cooler wind, laced with light rain begins to gust and whip the water. As fast as it appears, it's gone, leaving a calm, sunny idyllic scene for Gillet to catch his breath.

He is hungry. He needs rest, but as the wind picks back up, he knows he needs to eke miles out while he can. Having wind back, however, means the return of uncomfortable nights. Gillet is immediately reminded of the shortcoming of his backup-tarp cockpit cover when his stabilized sleeping kayak yaws on its sea anchors and water floods into his cocoon. *At least it's warmer*, he tries to comfort himself, *piece of cake compared to the first few weeks.* His partially dried-out sleeping bag grows bulkier again, turning back into a sponge. Gillet pops half a Halcion to aid in maximizing his soaked rest.

At dawn on Day 36, Gillet rouses, musty and crusty, to assess the wind. In the same breath that he sits up onto his saltwater sores, he notices the empty spot on the deck: *No drybag! Oh no. Must be overboard!!* Gillet quickly breaks down his pontoons, ties down the anchors and readies for the search. The bag is his kitchen, containing both of his cooking pots, the better of his two propane stoves, and most critically, all the instant coffee.

Each minute searching becomes more deflating. He scans methodically downwind, squinting and scouring, hoping to spot the deep-blue bag still bobbing between waves. *Why did I choose a blue bag?* The self-loathing continues as Gillet kicks himself for the seemingly unconscious choice to stow both pans in the same bag. The isn't good for morale. After two hours, he gives up on the hunt and changes his gears from paddling recon for the bag to fishing for calories. This raises another question sans stove: *How will I cook a fish if I catch one? And how to rehydrate any of the freeze-dried meals?* He stops to dig up and revive his one spare stove, getting more corroded by the day. To improvise a pot, he cuts off the top of a steel fuel canister. Handle? His on-board pliers. A plastic water bottle cut in half constitutes his new bowl.

This still doesn't solve his coffee problem. Since the high-mileage, high-intensity Baja expedition with Landick, Gillet got hooked not only on caffeine delivered in coffee, but also caffeine itself—popping pills to make extra miles on empty stomachs with exhausted limbs. Whether or not the caffeine was actually burning fatty acids, as he was told, instead of muscle glucose, the science didn't really matter. What he now knows is that the pills alter his mood for the better, stabilize fatigue levels, and boost his sense of alertness, not to mention overall motivation. With only fifteen Vivarin tablets, however, he knows he has to be choosy. This kitchen bag situation is not necessarily critical. And given the frenzied search, he is pretty awake. The wind is blowing enough to fly the kite and make a little downwind progress, so he saves a caffeine-tablet ration for later. Groggy will have to do.

He immediately regrets the choice. Going through the motions for his noon sun sighting, Gillet stashes the sextant in its waterproof case and then, while rotating around to wedge the case behind his seat, somehow fumbles it overboard. *Not good.* He loses sight of the dull-gray case as it separates from the kayak. Gillet scrambles to secure the kite line to a deck cleat, letting it fly free before hitting the water some fifty yards downwind—*it shouldn't be as hard to find later as the case now.* He cranks the boat around 180 degrees, scans the water again. He starts paddling furiously back against the wind. After only a hundred yards, he spots and snags it, kicking himself: *Come on! There can be no room for error*, he reprimands himself as he catches his breath, then locates and grabs the downed kite.

The next day, in place of his coffee, Gillet reflects on how that simple lapse with the sextant case could have snowballed into a fatal turning point. For his morning sighting, he opens the case, imbuing the sextant with a new layer of importance. He must stay vigilant and ever aware. Pulling out the three-pound plastic device, he reflects on the one positive of this long stretch in the purgatory of dead-calm waters: At least the now-flat ruler's edge of the horizon allows him to realign the sextant's mirrors that had warped slightly in the bustle of breaking through the frigid and relentless onshore orbit.

With the sextant corrected, he focuses keenly on all the steps involved in a sighting. First, he holds the twelve-inch quarter-circle of an instrument up to his eye, looking into the back-side telescope eyepiece at the front horizon mirror. This coated mirror is semitransparent, allowing him to peer straight through to the water's edge horizon, while also seeing the reflection up to the index mirror. This secondary upper mirror is mounted on an arm that Gillet can adjust, sliding it along the indexed outer arc of the device with his left hand. Gillet unclamps the arm, adjusting the shaded index mirror up and down to locate the sun in the sky. The sun's reflection through the index mirror shows up as a small disk of light on the horizon mirror. As Gillet pulls the sliding arm, he drops the reflected disk down onto the horizon that he sees. With the bottom of the disk resting on the horizon, Gillet clamps the arm down, allowing him to read the measurement—that is, the celestial object's angle of elevation, in degrees from the horizon. Because Gillet is essentially at the surface of the water, there's no need to correct for his own elevation as he would do from a ship's deck. Then he makes note of the exact time.

For good measure, Gillet repeats the whole process four more times. He takes the average of the five sights to correct for any drastically outlying variations. Then Gillet enters his final number and his time into a program on the navigation calculator, which takes account of the sun's declination and hour angle (according to hardwired astronomical data) and solves the spherical trigonometry formulas to generate a single longitudinal line of position—an estimate of how many degrees west Gillet lies of an imaginary zero-degree meridian line running from the North Pole through the Royal Observatory in Greenwich, England, to the South Pole. To estimate how far his kayak has drifted west overnight, he simply advances that line of position from the last sighting (and longitudinal line of position generated) on the afternoon prior. But that still gives him a sense of his latitude, or distance north of the equator, as well as the Hawaiian Island chain. To fix his position along that advancing line of north-south longitude, Gillet shoots the sun at its noon-hour high point to establish a perpendicular, east-west line of position. Where those two lines cross provides an updated latitude-longitude location that he writes down in the journal on the final day of July, his thirty-seventh day at sea.

Despite his cravings to hold a warm mug of coffee, he at least feels a little relief comparing the number to the day prior: He made seventy-four miles after losing the kitchen bag and its precious caffeinated contents! Katie would surely be proud of him back home tracking the Argos data.

The elation is short lived. When he plugs the number into his navigation calculator relative to his destination, Hilo, it also tells him the distance remaining, which doesn't paint a cheery bigger picture. He isn't even halfway there. And now, there is no more 30-130. Only Hilo, at just below 20 degrees north latitude and nearly another 20 degrees west, still ahead of him, at 155.

It's only numbers, he reassures himself. *Simply a running tally, an argument of position I've been building over the days. Information to pace myself and a course to steer, nothing more.* He does his final calculation, generating a "course made good" heading direction, which jibes with the "course to steer" compass heading that he's been using. He hasn't been drifting much off his course. He just needs to keep paddling and not think about the larger numbers.

That afternoon, a mahi strikes his trolling line. As it starts to run, Gillet stashes his paddles and wraps the line to a deck cleat. *This fish has some size.* He simply hopes it will start to wear itself out as it pulls the kayak sideways, tugging on the three-hundred-pound-test tuna cord. *Again,* he reminds himself of the morning's lesson as he slowly reels it in, *no errors here.* Gillet stays extra conscious of his hands—his crucial motor—as he pulls his worn-out catch near the kayak. Using a small gaff to pull the thrashing thirty-pound fish over his cockpit, he takes great care not to puncture his neoprene spraydeck, or worse, to snag the triple treble-hooked lure on a finger.

He grabs it by the gills, wrapping one arm under its yellowish sides. The mahi's tail slaps Gillet's ear, the writhing bright gold body knocking his gaff overboard. He sees it sink away momentarily as the fish slows its flailing. Gillet hugs it tight in celebration, taking a moment to appreciate the fish's stunning colors: a dorsal fin pocked by iridescent gold flakes sparkling with light blue dots on a bright green back; such a different look in hunting mode than the docile mahi casually accompanying his kayak with more silvery sides and darker blue backs.

As the colors fade, he goes to quick work cleaning, gutting, and boning, producing nearly twenty pounds of quivering pink filets. He carefully pulls out one of the dried-out matches and lights the backup stove. *Success!* Gillet boils the filets in ocean water. He mouths the first sweet, warm bite, kicking his head back in ecstasy. The flavor is so foreign to taste buds growing used to weeks of freeze-dried cardboard. He can't get enough. He can't even wait to boil the meat; he starts eating the filets raw. After two hours of chewing and five pounds of fish, he comes up for air. His belly actually feels full. It's a strange sensation coupled with a strong headache. He needs to stop gorging to keep something for later, and more bait for the next catch.

Prior to mounting the Hawaii trip, Gillet had consumed Steve Callahan's book *Adrift* just as voraciously. The nine-month 1986 best seller catalogues Callahan's solo survival experience floating west across the Atlantic in a life raft after his sailboat struck an object and sank. A lot of Callahan's observations and outlook sank in with Gillet. Looking at his mahi surplus, Gillet immediately recalls Callahan's diagrams of stretching out his fish catches by line-drying filets of the mahi he caught (referring to the colorful and curious pelagic game fish by its other common Spanish-derived name, dorado).

Without a line, or even points to hang the filets from, Gillet opts for sun-drying them on the deck. With each splash negating hours of dehydrating effort, however, the mounting smell of rotting fish forces Gillet to abandon the tactic. With the full belly, Gillet takes physical stock of himself, pushing his legs off the water bladder to still feel a bit of muscle below. The wind is still favorable enough to fly his kite 45 degrees off the wind to stay on course. Progress. *We're OK.* "Just hang on and not miss the islands," he writes in the journal.

By Day 38, he's back to freeze-dried fare. And cold eats too, hoping to minimize stove use and keep risk of corrosion and failures triggered by overuse at bay. The shortwave radio goes silent again. This time, however, the freshwater rinse-and-dry doesn't work. The colors leaking out look strange and smell corrosive. There's not even a hint of static, no matter how hard he hits the case with the back of his hand. Gillet gives it a proper burial, at sea, watching it sink away, imagining the distance it has to travel, nearly three miles down into the dark and silent primordial ooze far, far below. Tubeworms left to make sense of the plastic device.

On the surface, it's now silent as well. No more human voices. His Radio Shack weather radio is all that's left. It's used for listening in to any weather warnings, but mainly to check his watches against the WWV signal, where the US National Institute of Standards and Technology continuously transmits the time on multiple carrier frequencies. The spliced together time entries of a recorded male voice—generated from a computer in Fort Collins, Colorado—don't exactly count for company. Except after five weeks of hearing the same baritone robo-voice, when Gillet tunes in, something is different. The voice does matter. It's a new voice, the siren call of a female robot.

This means that the signal is now stronger and coming from the NIST's signal transmitting Coordinated Universal Time from its secondary station in Kauai. The voice makes the destination real again, and Gillet revels again in his daily task, absorbing the smallest actions in his strokes, splashing as he looks out "over purple plains."

Wide open spaces, deserts, and plains are the only parallels worth drawing to his surroundings. The ocean has a more empty, sterile feel than one harboring unknown predators and mysterious creatures in the dark abyss. They must be down there somewhere, but the depths feel bottomless, without any apparent ecosystem or reason to reside there. None of the other life is threatening. Everything is moving. Like him, every pelagic creature he encounters is on the move, headed somewhere else, with a better place to go.

With the shade that his kayak provides, Gillet starts to appreciate that he is becoming that better place. Hints of a unique drifting ecosystem begin forming around him. Flying fish herald his approach to new sections of waters. Broad-winged terns fly ahead of the kayak, picking off fish. Dolphins appear in the distance, but busy wrangling tuna, they swim off, uninterested in the entourage of sea life accompanying the kayak. Mahi are the only fish that approach the kayak directly. The swift and sleek predators charge out ahead like sentinels, then return to glide alongside the boat, schooling underneath it at night.

Gillet can start to recognize the return of individuals by their distinct spot patterns. *These fish are capable of forty knots*, Gillet wonders, *why are they traveling with me?* The connections to these mysterious creatures start to become personal, like a child drawn to a comforting stray dog. The layers of emotional attachment become strained by Gillet's appetite.

In an attempt to understand their thinking and condition them to swim closer to the kayak, he knocks on the hull before throwing them spare bait chunks of his previous catch. Throughout the day, he continues the chore of knocking and tossing over free food. After two days and dwindling bait, hoping to have drilled in the association, knock-to-food, he tosses in a lure. A mahi hits it instantly! Gillet can feast again.

He's also taking more than his fill with the favorable conditions. "A kite-paddler's dream" is the only way he can label the warm days filled with constant wind. He gets in a rhythm: Wake and immediately launch kite; start steering with the rudder, munching down a cold breakfast of peanut butter and granola bar while securing the floats and anchors. Then, start slowly adding paddle power. It reminds him of the fast kite-paddling he'd done in the Southern Ocean, gaining steadfast confidence in this system, cruising up to seven knots along the central coast of Chile.

No need for a cumbersome sailing rig, one that in Gillet's experience trying to implement onto a kayak never worked out well anyway. Not only was a sail only effective in light-to-moderate winds from one direction, but open-ocean swells would render it useless, interfering with the surface winds, blowing on the crests and dying in the troughs. A mast-and-sail rig would also mess with his stroke, and transform his sleek and efficient rough-water craft into an awkwardly inept sailboat. Paddling with the extra boost of the kite flying seventy-five feet up keeps him occupied and in the present, focused on the wave ahead. The downwind hours add up, fourteen, fifteen, sixteen, seventeen a day. Gillet looks back at the blur of five days covering 280 miles, a pace of fifty-six miles a day.

On Day 46, it ends. The winds die again. Not having that extra tug is demoralizing, suddenly missing that colorful high-flying extra object to absorb his attention and make the hours fly by. The hours start to stretch as Gillet returns to the slog. He must paddle to keep moving. The second he stops, he begins to burn calories without forward progress. He starts thinking too much. The anxiety spikes and then simmers, mental peaks and valleys instead of the welcome ups and downs of wind-driven waves. He begins mulling over a new choice he feels he's barreling toward making: ask for rescue, or starve in the boat. All he can do to stop thinking is to keep paddling. By hour sixteen, he knows his body needs rest, but he does not want to stop. The only way to reconcile the need to rest is to pop a Halcion to quiet his mind.

The next four days, the calm seas and stormy thoughts continue. He starts to recognize the onset of the anxiety spikes. He can't even paddle at their peak. Debilitated, he slumps in his seat, the tears well up from nowhere, erupting in sobs for uncontrollable minutes, surrendering to the emotion that captures every bit of his attention. Then it passes and his mood immediately improves. He regains the grip on his thoughts and again on his paddle, beginning to get his boat back up to speed and on its course south and west.

The rapid swings are not going unnoticed. Gillet tries to observe what's happening. He chalks up the attacks to the basic situational intensity, the accumulation of exhaustion and stress. But he begins to problem solve, starting with realizing these feelings are simply episodes to weather. He needs to come up with solutions to cope. *It's OK*, Gillet tells himself as he hews to a mantra, *Tomorrow is another day, just paddle a little more.*

Even as he tries to reign in his attention, signs of increased desperation and loneliness creep into his journal. He describes Day 49 in sparse terms, simply a "very bad day emotionally." The mahi seem to be on to him too, paying no attention to his lures. He rehydrates his last piece of meat, some freeze-dried pork chops, and uses a scrap to somehow catch a four-foot mahi. After slicing off everything edible, he reaches some scraps back overboard. Some of the mahi eat pieces of their brethren straight from Gillet's hand. He won't starve as long as they keep him company, so he keeps dropping them morsels, in a way returning the favor. He splits his fresh fish rations to keep them interested, not only because he values their company, but because he understands just how much he needs them for survival.

The anxiety comes roaring back under a scorching midday sun. The choice to rest or paddle feels loaded with extra pressure. Life or death? Sink or swim? The two choices become an active decision from one moment to the next. He must consciously pick between sanity and going mad. This is a far deeper test of self than he ever bargained for. Gillet makes a vow, signing a compact with himself: *If I make it to Hawaii, I will never talk about my crossing.*

This one is different, he thinks. The South America experience, that one was worth talking about—the warm people plus the few hostile ones, the amazing coastline unspooling under strange stars. That tale was cut from the same cloth as Paul Theroux's *The Old Patagonian Express* or Yvon Chouinard's account of the 1968 "Fun Hog" road trip from California to the Patagonian summit of Fitz Roy: a story of freedom and serendipity in total commitment, where things always seem to work out. Even in pain, there was joy. This, now, feels darker, more desperate, and much more foolhardy. Life or death. Sane or mad. Sink or swim. The challenge is too close, the vision quest too spiritual. *These thoughts must stay a secret. To talk about this would be a betrayal.*

The return of the trade winds offers a day of mental reprieve—surfing ten-foot swells in the middle of the ocean, waiting for mahi to hit his line. The break is tempered on Day 54 with a thought to switch things up, breaking out of a mental balancing act that has become too routine: *Escape the confines of the cabin!* Gillet decides to inspect the outside of the kayak.

With warm enough water, he skips the wet suit and just slides over the edge. It comes as a shock when he sinks. His buoyant body fat is gone. His legs slice through the water as he struggles to stay at the surface. Finally, he dives under the kayak to inspect, surprised again at the sight of the fore and aft sections of his hull, covered in a thick carpet of sponges, barnacles, and algae. The only clear area is between the cockpits, rubbed smooth by the webbing straps he's been running underneath to secure the pontoon tubes. No wonder the mahi are so interested in his kayak and the baitfish procession it must attract. After cleaning sailboat hulls for three years, and having packed a scraper, he should have known. Gillet regrets not painting on a heavy coat of anti-fouling paint—a choice that he made, ironically, for the sake of keeping the fiberglass hull smooth and reducing any extra drag. Now all he's doing is dragging a small community of organisms with every stroke. He also knows the effort it will take at this point to remove all the algae growth.

The boat is becoming too comfortable at rest. The ocean is becoming too connected to the craft. And he to it. Separating himself from it momentarily, he acknowledges how his body has changed as he kicks feverishly to keep afloat: This is a wake-up call. *Get back to business.* All effort needs to be directed at making distance. *Let's move.*

No extra energy is expended in his navigation process either, which is becoming more streamlined. Gillet sticks to the three daily sun sightings to establish his "running fix," in the morning around 10 a.m., at "local noon" and then again at 4 p.m. For quicker recall each morning of the previous day's position, hoping to assess his drift overnight, Gillet simplifies the process of "informed dead reckoning" via a single daily position estimate: He scrawls the numbers directly onto the yellow deck of the kayak with a grease underwater-marking pencil.

At his noon sight, he gets another surprise. Using the measurement to calculate his daily position fix, his new number is thirty miles above his established course. He's getting quickly pushed too far north—above the closest landing spot on the Big Island. The anxiety begins building again. Questions gnaw: *Am I steering north? Is there a north current? Should I have stayed farther south, hugging my boundary with the southern tropical storm track?*

He can't think about the weather. He has to abandon the bigger picture after wishing and hoping and praying for wind—only for it to blow him north, up and over instead of down onto his island landing point. Yet when he tries to avoid the dread by honing into his immediate little oceanic world, the frames shift right back to food. A mental inventory of food he's already parsed only gets him lost in the same loop: flashbacks of the deck-bound bagels, vivid fantasies of every type of fare, meals long forgotten, even salivating over the thought of SPAM. *Maybe a vessel will pass. I wish for a ship to pass so I can beg for food.*

"Same ocean, different numbers," Gillet scrawls in his journal on Day 55. "Food remaining is 4 days if I continue to ration and eat as little as possible. No guarantee that I'll make Hawaii in 4 or 5 days—at least 280 miles to go."

He's skipping meals altogether—down to five hundred calories a day. Rations supplemented by a midday caffeine tablet. After his afternoon sun sighting, he scratches the day's new position—22° 20' N, 150° 40' W—onto the hull like a prisoner etching days onto the wall of his cell. The passing ship that he wishes for never appears. He does somehow manage to conjure a Styrofoam cup that seemingly appears from nowhere—must have been thrown from a nearby cruise ship. He paddles over and snags it, noticing a dark ring of coffee dried in the bottom. He whips out his stove and doesn't hesitate using it today. Pouring the hot water with shaking hands into the cup like a heroin junkie handling a hot spoon, Gillet rehydrates the coffee remnant and drinks it down. *So good!*

There's no more luck catching the few fish below. They are onto his knocking trick, and without a line trolling at a decent speed, the mahi won't take his lures. Sitting and fishing, not paddling to his target only makes Gillet more agitated and desperate. Paddling is the only thing that keeps the anxiety attacks at bay. But even with each stroke, a panicked thought—of the dragging hull or of overexerting and burning too many calories—begins to creep into his more relaxed headspace typically lost in habitual motion and action. He decides to toss out any extra unnecessary weight in the boat, starting with two hefty items originally meant to help quiet his mind. For the first time all trip, he pulls out the stashed anthology of poetry and his copy of *The Odyssey*. Without a second thought he tosses them overboard.

Before dusk he spots a black frigate. The sight is more than welcome, as Gillet knows that a frigate can only be a single day's flight from land, where they spend their nights. What does appear regularly in the night sky also torments him about his relative proximity to a destination that he is slowly drifting above: that is, the silent blinking lights of commercial aircraft. He visualizes the passengers' beige tray tables chocked full of pineapple chicken portions, overcooked rice, a wilted salad, carrot cake dessert topped by sweet canned frosting. He can smell the packaged meal as the flight attendant rumbles the cart down the aisle toward his seat.

Gillet adjusts his seat, sliding back onto a terrible sore on his butt. He slithers off of it, down into the cockpit, still thinking of that carrot cake. He prays for northeast wind. He prays for a fish bite. He folds the rolled end of the hydrocortisone tube and thumbs out the last spreadable smidge of cream onto the backs of his throbbing hands. His pops a Halcion pill and eventually sleep subdues his thoughts.

Light winds from the east awake Gillet before first light. Not boisterous by any means, but enough to fly the kite. He needs to get south.

He focuses all his attention away from food, away from anything but the next stroke, each movement an expression of his will to hold fast to a 235-degree heading. He keeps the pressure on himself, paddling and holding fast for the next seventeen hours.

"Shit," Gillet writes upon waking the next day and measuring his progress, his fifty-seventh at sea, "only came down 10 miles since yesterday."

"TEN MILES!!" he screams into the sky. Because the Hawaiian Islands run northwesterly up from the Big Island, the higher Gillet's latitude, the longer it will take to make landfall as he continues to veer farther west. If he can hold a course steering as closely to southwest as possible, he would still need another 230 miles to hit Maui. Except he can't hold this course. Extrapolating his positions based on the northward current of the last couple of days, Gillet estimates a landing on Oahu, 316 miles away—maybe even missing the islands completely. An optimistic Oahu landing in Kaneohe Bay, in food terms, means at least an additional three days travel past the closing window on Maui.

He looks down at the choppy, gray waters stirred up by the northern current mirrored by hazy grayish skies. The mahi school is long gone, off to chase faster fish in bluer waters. Gillet starts imagining how it will feel when his body starts to starve and shut down physiologically, which organs will fail first. As his depressed emotions enter full tailspin, more religious answers percolate from forgotten depths—full prayers memorized in parochial school and compartmentalized in memory stores for the last three decades. Gillet recites lost poetry and random passages recalled from Caesar's *Gallic War*.

The time continues to pass. Gillet can only shift his bony butt, hold onto that southwest course, crunch through a few cold bites of flavorless rehydrated food, and keep paddling. Though the backs of his hands are cracked and blistered, his calloused palms feel strong, and another sixteen hours of paddling keep the tailspin from bottoming out.

The winds on Day 58 shift slightly. For the worse. They're blowing even more from the southeast. The kite cannot fly on his opposing heading southwest to 230 degrees. He begins spinning out again. He's going to miss the islands. He's running out of food and he can only stay sane if he is burning calories. His body is deteriorating. There are no more fat reserves to burn. No more antibiotics to stave off infection. No more caffeine tablets for fuel.

He can't keep paddling on this course. Exhausted, he stops paddling, and keeps drifting north. *I'm going to die. I'm sure that I will not make it.* He imagines the fishing boat approaching the drifting yellow contraption, loose lines blowing in the wind, only to find Gillet's lifeless body inside. He imagines Katie hearing the news back at the shop. Tears start rolling down his face. He pulls out his pencil, hand shaking.

"Hands very cracked and swollen. Maybe diet related," he pauses. Then continues writing. "Maybe should write a will here: Everything I have goes to my wife Kathleen Kampe, who I love deeply. Katie, I'm sorry for causing you so much grief and pain."

Exploring this new personal low for a few minutes after writing the will, Gillet starts to feel better. He sits back up, grabs for his paddle and starts moving once again through the overcast day. He attempts any progress through gray, barren waters, devoid of fish or bird life. The anxiety attacks seem to be more potent, and happening more frequently, passing along as rapidly as their sudden onset, almost coming from something outside himself.

He skips the Halcion that night. No hope for sleep, his mind continues to sound alarms about missing the islands. Gillet tries to spin positives. That NOAA forecast earlier on the weather radio, after all, came through from the station signal on Mauna Kea, the high point on Big Island. That's only 170 miles! Don't think about the bad news: that the forecaster was warning of a tropical depression set to continue the "Kona winds," from a southerly direction, for the next twenty-four to forty-eight hours. He wonders about what that low-flying aircraft was doing. He couldn't see it through the haze, but could imagine it air-dropping fresh Chips Ahoy! cookies. Thinking about treats brings him back to the dread of his empty food inventory. The words he last wrote in his journal echo as waves lap against the hull: "Feel like a condemned man."

It's time, he thinks. He grabs his pliers and shimmies up the kayak. Straddling the bow, he reaches in to grab the blaze orange tube from the nose of the hull. Pulling out the Argos unit, he inspects the exposed jumper wire and recalls his deal with Katie: If he cuts the main wire, the temperature data goes on and the signal will be read, "Watch me closely." It is the same subtext as if they were climbing a rock wall together: pull the slack out of the rope and hold on—this could go wrong fast. Should Gillet choose to cut the wire, then a simple pull of the pin on his EPIRB device would be all that was necessary to send the secondary message of final resort: "Emergency, send rescue."

Gillet takes a deep breath and feels the full weight of his decision to alter his single lifeline.

He snips the jumper wire.

Steve Landick takes a rare rest with local fishermen off Boca San Juanico during his and Gillet's thirty-day, nine hundred–mile blitz down Baja California's Pacific Coast from San Diego to Cabo San Lucas in late 1982.

Call of the Wild: Gillet, age thirty-three, camping in Ecuador in late 1984 and nearing the end of his five thousand–mile odyssey up South America's west coast from Punta Arenas, Chile, to Ecuador's Colombian border—where he found out the hard way his need for a more remote trip to "the emptiest place I could imagine."

An unwieldy ten-pound PVC tube encased the bulky aluminum body of an Argos satellite transmitter (on loan from the Scripps Institution of Oceanography), an antenna, a ninety-day battery, and the jumper wire rigged to alter transmission. This functioned as Gillet's sole outbound communication tool.

After sewing the nylon webbing cradles on the drive up to Monterey Harbor, Gillet tests out his overnight stabilization system the day before departure by harnessing two duffel-sized rubber tubes (a pair of thwart cross-sections from a whitewater raft) astride the rear cockpit.

Two months after they married and three months after they opened a small business together, Ed Gillet and Katie Kampe say their goodbyes, budgeting forty days away (sixty max), which they promised to take "one day at a time."

Bright eyes and high hopes on Day 1: June 25, 1987. With extra food lashed on a deck laden in lines and gear, Gillet planned to remove the front domed lid, deploy sea anchors nested underneath, and then affix the lid over the rear cockpit at night. Life jacket? Wrapped around the foil-lined radar reflector pole rigged vertically in hopes of alerting passing ships.

Gillet's twenty-foot-long, thirty-one-inch-wide Necky Tofino rides low under the full weight of a six hundred–pound load.

The initial crux that dooms Trans-Pacific voyagers: the ever turbulent and hazardous lane where current and wind running down and toward the California coast conspire to lock travelers onshore. Gillet sets his sea anchor, visible on a seventy-five-foot line, before shimmying into his bivouac at sea, all while the kayak slides down the back of the fifteen-foot swell, wrenching on the anchor line and rendering sleep impossible.

After two punishing first weeks of wet and heavy exertion by day and tortured discomfort by night, with hours dissolving into "a fog of fatigue, pain, bone chilling cold, fear, and misery," Gillet makes a decision after his rudder snaps.

Are those trees? On Day 14 Gillet spots the USS *Ramsey* 450 miles west of San Diego, his last confirmed position.

Once the mahi's stunning, iridescent colors fade, Gillet goes to quick work cleaning, gutting, and boning his first catch, producing nearly twenty pounds of quivering pink filets that provide welcome relief to taste buds dulled by weeks of freeze-dried, cardboard-like fare.

Day 45: Gillet affixes the base of his Nikonos IV to a nut at the end of his paddle shaft to capture a warm day with constant wind. "A kite-paddler's dream" is the only way he can label a string of days covering fifty-plus miles a day, paddling up to seventeen hours a day. The conditions do not last.

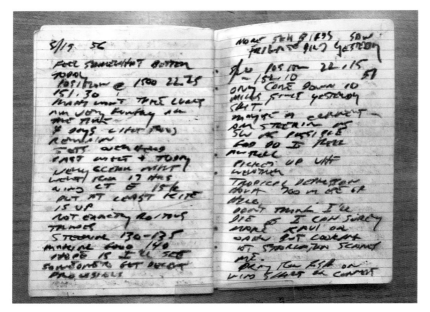

What If I Needed Help? - Gillet spells out the hard questions in all caps with a grease underwater-marking pencil in his journal, which starts as a navigation log but unspools into a catalog of haunting thoughts.

Gillet displays the balancing act of between-leg cooking on his spare stove. After losing his kitchen kit, he relies on pliers to handle a pot made from an old fuel canister. Note his position readings written directly onto the hull.

Navigation becomes visual as clouds piling up on the windward shore of Maui come into view, sixty miles from landfall.

After his 6 a.m. landing in Maui's Kahului Harbor on August 27, 1987, with no welcoming party and no elation, Gillet is in no rush to leave his kayak. With scarred, peeling hands, he sets the timer for one last self-portrait.

"I had absolutely no desire to be anywhere else or do anything different," Gillet said, reflecting on his surprise landing day after consuming twenty-two dollars worth of Häagen-Dazs and hotel commissary snacks. "Just sitting there completely at peace."

Outside the Maui Beach Hotel, Katie pulls out the errant Argos tube, along with all the empty refuse after her husband had consumed everything edible aboard his capsule.

Months after the Hawaii crossing, Katie and Ed took the trusty Tofino on a full transit of the Baja Peninsula, setting camp on the east side of Isla Angel de la Guarda.

CHAPTER NINE

Past Due

THE ARGOS UNIT HAS NOT SENT A SIGNAL IN FORTY-FIVE DAYS. NO DATA at all, location or temperature.

For the first nine days of the trip, the stashed bundle that constitutes the kayak's outbound communications works right to plan: the Scripps Institution receives the data signal and Russ Davis phones it over to Katie Kampe. At the Southwest Kayaks shop, Kampe maps each of the day's locations, up to the seeming anomaly of her husband turning back in toward the California coast. Then on July 4, the signal stops. Alone at the shop, Kampe rings in her Fourth of July with unwanted internal fireworks. She weighs all the options: Ed has either dropped it overboard and, without the buoys of the other Argos transmitters, it has likely sunk; or he has sunk. Or maybe he'd run into something. Maybe something horrific has happened. Maybe.

Davis has no information. "I was afraid we had done something wrong and made the transmitter fail," he recalls. "No such unit had ever failed for us."

Kampe maintains faith in her husband's abilities for another three more days. She refuses to catastrophize. *He just threw it overboard*, she reasons. *Easy to do in a kayak.* Still, she can't help but glimpse at the other, worse, options. They percolate up with each unnerving conclusion to the daily calls to Scripps that yield a blank response from Davis and the researchers monitoring for the signal. Then on July 8, marking the start of Gillet's second week at sea, the signal comes on again—just prior to his run-in with the USS *Ramsey* in the Naval convoy that presumably detunes the Argos unit's oscillator. Kampe records the location, which has her husband back on his course south and a little west. All must be well. For after this lone signal transmission, the Argos stops working for good.

This gives Katie enough information to rest easy: One, Ed is headed to Hawaii; two, this is exactly what he predicted. If electronics can fail, they will.

"I went, 'That's just electronic,'" she recalls. "Ed warned me about this countless times. He had told me, 'If you take this stuff on board something is going to happen, and you're going to think I'm dead if I can't talk to you, and really the worst that's happened is that everything electronic has gone out.'"

Of course he wasn't turning around, Kampe affirms. She throws herself back into the business: fixing the trailer assembly wiring on the van, ordering additional kayaks, and even collecting slips from the shop's closest friends for a lottery to help cover some of the Hawaii trip costs: guess Ed's arrival date and win a piece of gear off the kayak! She is making the situation work, handling the shop stress with Alex's help, and carrying the emotional weight of uncertainty with trust in all her husband's preparation and confidence. She can handle the pressure, she likes to say, again pointing to the mold cast by her father, the decorated colonel, "because I lived in a pressure cooker being my father's daughter!"

Gillet's family, however, is not coping as well with the communication blackout. Ed Gillet Sr., then working as a Pensacola, Florida-based, air traffic controller, calls his daughter Catherine in New York every day after the transmitter signal stops. Catherine can't help but wonder about her beloved older brother, the one who used to ride her to school in the basket of his bike. She has to try *something.* She comes up with an idea, recalling a conversation with Ed after his Inside Passage trip where he had told her that he listened to the radio throughout the entire trip. Having grown up admiring his intellect, and following in his steps as an academic high achiever, comparing favorite reads and recommended films to one another, she knew that *All Things Considered* was her big brother's favorite program.

"I thought, well, it's worth a try, so I called the National Public Radio number in Washington, D.C., and asked to speak with a producer," says Catherine Gillet, who was eventually patched through. The show staffer was receptive and took in all the info on her brother's situation, plus the request to broadcast a message for the missing kayaker to "phone home" by activating his EPIRB at a specific time. "All kinds of things were going through our heads of where he might be and maybe he was rescued by a tanker or a ship. I wanted to let him know we were thinking of him and loved him and wishing him a safe journey and send a basic message to 'Please Call.'"

The producer ingests the news tip and offers to follow the story. The request for the message, however, never makes it to the air. Not that it would have been heard anyway. At the point, over a week had passed since Gillet's radio settled to the bottom of six thousand feet of water.

Gillet's parents and sisters start calling Kampe with the increased urgency of every passing day. Without concrete updates or positive news, the conversations fray. Fingers start pointing. When the worst is assumed, Kampe's role is questioned in perhaps pushing her partner away on a final voyage. Desperation and hostility define the tense interactions. Gillet Sr. needs action.

"He was fighting every day, trying to get someone to rescue my brother," Catherine says. "Which I think is what parents do, but certainly my father was doing everything."

On August 15—Gillet's fifty-second day at sea, and the date his family had circled as a projected landing date, erring on a couple of days past the midpoint of Gillet's original projected trip-duration range of forty to sixty days—Gillet Sr. puts in repeat calls to the Coast Guard to mount a rescue. Though they're received and processed through the right channels, they only result in a query for more information. The Coast Guard doesn't have much frame of reference for a Pacific Ocean kayaking transit so they contact David Burch, the Seattle kayaker, navigation author, and instructor, to evaluate potential search areas or locations.

"What I did was develop a polar diagram that figured out what wind speeds and angles he could potentially sail, and what he had to paddle," Burch says. "Then I got the latest information every day from NOAA about the state of the wind and the sea and I would make an estimated route, with uncertainties of where he could be."

Burch works day and night. "It was a lot of work," he says. "This all had to be done by hand, on weather charts and open-ocean sea state charts and it was really tedious." Starting with Gillet's last confirmed position—more than a month prior during his communication with the USS *Ramsey* 450 miles west of San Diego—Burch builds the likely route, "assuming he [kite-]sails when he can and paddles when he can." And each day, Burch continues an ongoing route position projection. As Burch gets more data with each new day, the position moves a little bit. The radius of the uncertainty, his "error circle" gets a little bigger.

But only by a small margin. As Burch pulls the data, he notices particularly mild wind patterns. The conditions aren't expanding the radius of his error circle much. It raises an immediate question: Was Gillet in fact late? No. He communicates his findings to his Coast Guard contact in Long Beach, California.

The case for rescue was weak. "Virtually impossible" is how Charlie Crosby, a Coast Guard spokesman, describes the lack of even an approximation of where to look, adding that, should Gillet be off course, "he could be in an area approximately one-and-a-half times the size of the continental United States, and that's the minimum area."

The *Los Angeles Times* reporter who gets the word from the Coast Guard also speaks with Kampe, who seeks to temper the building hysteria by reaffirming the research of Burch, the sea kayaking mutual-friend connection, and his inspection of satellite pictures illustrating the flat, calm conditions missing the regular trade winds. She also falls back on her confidence in Gillet's competence, finishing the interview by telling the reporter how she still supports her husband's trip. "It's never a question of putting up with [his travel]," she says. "That's who I married and why I married him."

To help calm others without that trust—others who doubted the trip, or imagined the worst—Kampe also revises the projected arrival date for the record. Though Gillet gave himself a maximum of sixty days, she expands the buffer to September 6, adding on an additional two weeks. She hopes that will quell some of the building panic, and, with it, any other media inquiries.

Meanwhile, the limited search-and-rescue effort seems off the table after Capt. Galene R. Siddall, the ranking chief of the Eleventh Coast Guard District's Search and Rescue Division in Long Beach, California, also refuses to issue an overdue report. "The humanitarian gesture would be to make the effort to search and make everyone feel better," he responds. "But if we launched every time we had a request, we'd be out of funds." The Coast Guard does at least make a conciliatory offer to broadcast on certain frequencies to reach Gillet as well as to broadcast notices to all mariners and aviators in the broad target area to report any kayaker sightings.

That's not going to work for Ed Gillet Sr. The day that his son desperately snips the wire on his Argos system, Gillet Sr. pulls any strings he can, leaning heavily on his contacts with the navy. But like the Coast Guard, they deem a full-scale search unrealistic. Gillet Sr. still manages to send word out to some naval pilots in Hawaii. He even pushes his rescue request up the chain, contacting the US Coast Guard commandant in Washington, D.C., and finally types up and submits a plea via telegram to President Reagan himself. "I cannot believe my son will be left to die without some effort made to find him," he writes. "I am desperate and need your help. Each day my son's situation grows more dangerous. Please help us."

Though his high-level requests fail to result in meaningful rescue action, they do send newsworthy ripples through media outlets. The sourcing of information regarding Gillet's whereabouts and the reasoning regarding the denial of his rescue leads the press right to Burch.

"It got really nasty," Burch said. "There were three to four big papers, from D.C., in Seattle, papers in San Diego somewhere, and these guys were giving me hell, a horrible time."

A San Diego news station reaches out to Kampe as well with an additional interview request. She even gets called by Gillet Sr.'s hometown newspaper in Pensacola, Florida. "Kayaker lost at sea" stories began to appear in the press.

By Day 60, over a week past his ETA of August 15, Kampe has had it. As her levels of hostility rise with each high-pressure call from insensitive press members or irritated in-laws, she leaves town, driving north to pick up a couple of ordered kayaks in San Francisco. She knows that her husband must be out of food. Her stressed patience has worn thin, simply awaiting positive arrival news—or perhaps a much worse update. Back up at Bob Licht's Sea Trek outfit, she loads up the kayaks and calls the Coast Guard. Officials stationed in Hawaii, however, refuse to look for Gillet. She relays their explanation to Licht: "They told me, 'We'll never be able to find him, he's an ant,'" Kampe says.

"I asked Bob, 'What do I do?'" she says. "And he just said, 'There's nothing you can do.' There's nothing you can realistically do at that point and accomplish anything."

"I think it was hard on her," recalled Licht of the couple of tense days spent at his Sausalito shop, huddled around the radio for weather updates. "She was very concerned about him, she was very much in love with him and very much wanted him to come back. I think that was hard on her and I think she suffered."

With the search denied, Kampe drove back to San Diego with a load of sea kayaks and a heavy heart. Sixty days wasn't just her own personal cutoff date. The word on Gillet being "overdue" was officially out in the press and in the mind of the public. Messages awaited her arrival back at the shop, not just from panicked family and unknown reporters, but also from friends, forcing Kampe to dance around morbid questions and redouble her steadfast commitment to the belief her husband was fine.

"It was a very bad period," said Russ Davis, one of the worried kayak-shop friends who had wanted to make Gillet's trip safer with the inclusion of his lab's Argos device. He could feel some of the watchers' frustration, having promised an ability to track Gillet and field a potential distress signal. Now he shared Kampe's concern with an added layer of dejected personal responsibility, somehow complicit in the dire unknowns with the unit's failure. He could only describe that overdue atmosphere one way: "Despair was on the horizon."

— ❦ —

22° 15' North, 154° 05' West
Pacific Ocean
August 23

As Day 60 arrives for Gillet, he wakes to winds. *Headwinds! Jesus!* He channels the anger into strokes, cranking his heading to 260 degrees, right into the east-southeast wind. The breeze is crisp enough to drive wind-driven waves over the deck, often breaking all the way back into his cockpit. It's like paddling upriver. Gillet only stops paddling when a flying fish following the wind lands right on his spraydeck. He eats it raw.

By dusk he calculates latitude, scribbling numbers onto his deck, hoping he has made some progress south. The degrees north of the equator are not going down. He's drifted five miles north. His run? Only fifteen miles, his weakest daily total yet. As he drifts northwest, getting no closer to the islands, he imagines a spacecraft attempting to reenter the atmosphere at too shallow an angle, skipping off into the void. His thoughts drift away too. *Will the panic attacks become debilitating? How much more headwind paddling can I do without food to refuel?*

Fuel remains in his thoughts the next day as he eyes his last packaged meal—a foil pouch with stuffed cabbage rolls. He takes bites as small as possible, carefully mouthing the texture, attempting to extend his savor and extract flavor from the otherwise bland mush. As he slows to chew, he notices the jet streams in the clearing sky, converging tighter, lines closer in. He calculates his run from the day prior and corresponding latitude. *Ten miles south!*

He logs the position. "133 miles from Kahului, Maui. Trade winds return—Although not strong.

"Ate last meal this morning, BUT," he writes in all caps, then underlines it again, and again, and again, as he grapples with the implication, "noon sight brought good news. The current is stopped and I dropped 10 miles since yesterday. Tied kite shroud lines to keep angle to the wind and kite is working perfectly."

Though the seas are blue once again and he is moving in the right direction, he's still in desperate need. On Day 62 he scours the boat, upending drybags, searching for something—anything—to eat. He finds a lone tomato soup mix pack and stirs it in cold water with the last dust of his protein powder. For dessert, he puts a dab of his Colgate toothpaste on his finger and licks it off. The minty taste leads to another dab. And then another. He can't stop. Dab by dab he rolls the tube from the bottom and sucks its contents dry.

He paddles until 2 a.m. As exhaustion nears, he considers the stability pontoons. The inflation and cradle assembly would take at least a half hour and who knows how many calories. *Better to keep paddling and close the distance.* The closer he gets, the more desperate he is to reach the finish line. When he finally breaks, he doesn't bother with the pontoons. He slides in the cockpit, with the kayak nearly empty, riding high and buoyant in mellow waves and light winds.

After a morning on his sixty-third day waking and immediately claw-ing for miles, he itches for his noon sighting to validate his effort with another meaningful drop in latitude. He swings the sextant to the south-ern horizon. *Ugh, what the* fuck *is that? That mountain is screwing up the horizon.*

He takes a couple seconds to calibrate. *Mountain.*

He looks again. Unmistakable. Yes! A defined dark line. A plateau through the cloud layer of fluffy cumulus clouds. This must be the east shore of the Big Island. That must be a slice of the mountain—Mauna Kea—a glimpse offered through the trades piling up on the island's wind-ward side, obscuring the view of its 13,800-foot summit, the island chain's highest point.

This is real. A place with a name. All those numbers punched and scrawled, degrees and imaginary lines and constructs, they fade away. No more math, no more reckoning estimates. Gillet's perspective is shifting. He reaches for his camera to help frame this altered view. A physical target.

Except it's not his target. The Big Island is too far. He digs through his navigation drybag to find a stashed pilot chart for the Hawaiian Islands. Mauna Kea is eighty miles south. Maui should be only fifty miles ahead.

He stashes the map and paddles with renewed energy. As the squall above him passes, the view of the volcanic rim of the Haleakalā Crater, the ten thousand-foot top to Maui, comes into contrast. Navigation is now visual.

From this northerly approach to Maui, Gillet considers a landing in Hana on the eastern end of Maui's windward north side. That would mean a slight detour, however, backtracking east from his current course toward Pauwela Point in the middle of Maui's north shore. Speaking of detours, he imagines Katie, back in the shop, more keyed in now than ever to the Argos signal. Surely, she's seeing his approach to Maui and will need to change her flight from the Big Island.

By sunset, he can see the light on the point, which the cart indicates is visible within twenty-four miles. With each additional minute paddling, new details emerge: a blinking red antenna, dim shore lights. Energized,

Gillet paddles all night. A flying fish smacks him in the chest and lands on his deck. He brushes it off and keeps paddling.

As he cuts the distance in half, the sea changes. Rough and irregular wave patterns interrupt the long-period ocean swells that he's grown accustomed to. Whether reflecting off the island or mixing with currents around it, the new waves mean more challenges. Bruised, atrophied, and depleted, the backs of his hands seeping small amounts of blood with the tight-gripped strokes, Gillet must lock a scarred seat and sore legs back in for the heads-up brand of no-mistake paddling that marked the first two weeks of his journey.

Steep waves break over the kayak and slap Gillet in the chest, drenching him scalp to toe. Gillet grins. Eyes wide, he scans over the chaotic bumps with crazed attention set on the land mass ahead. The night sky begins to lighten along the eastern horizon over Gillet's left shoulder. He's paddling in such an aware state, one with his boat, that he stashes the paddle, riding the bubbly lumps with his foot-rudder in order to set up a self-portrait. He sets the timer and the flash, balancing the camera to mark the final day. *Steering for land!*

As the dawn of his sixty-fourth day approaches, Gillet rounds the point and makes his approach to Kahului Harbor. Paralleling the beach a few miles off the north shore of Maui, he can make out the car headlights of commuters taking the beach road into town. Maybe Katie is there, cruising the coast in a rental VW van, looking out for a lone kayaker. A foggy cap of clouds spills off the island. The offshore flow fills into the lee that Gillet has entered. The breeze envelops him, washing Gillet over in shockingly rich scents of loamy soil and flowery perfumes mixed with hints of car exhaust. This clear signal of verdant life overloads his saltwater-tuned senses. When his emotions catch up to the shock, Gillet tears up.

The aquatic gig is up. His strength and his supplies are gone. He's paddling a shell. His gear—the pontoon floats, kite, sea anchors, navigation books, sextant and calculator, sleeping bag, and watermaker—is all now loosely stowed amid a bunch of empty waterproof bags and bottles, spent fuel cartridges and plastic wrappers. *I've consumed everything edible aboard my little capsule*, Gillet thinks, comparing his fiberglass pod to a space traveler's. He knows he's lived too long off a limited life-support system. Depleted, on so many levels. Only the land can replenish body and spirit.

Paddling west looking for the harbor, Gillet starts thinking more practically. What about McDonald's? Is there one in Kahului? What time would it open? He's had his breakfast order planned long in advance. Five Egg McMuffins to go, please. What if there's a welcoming party? Maybe outrigger canoes to accompany him in! They'd surely have some kind of food before adorning him with leis. He spots a docked cruise ship marking the harbor entrance. Upon spotting it, he slows urgent strokes. The bright behemoth seems so foreign from his personal plastic eco-pod that he has integrated his life inside, and linked to on the outside, growing symbiotically with sea organisms along the way. Suddenly the end becomes real. Landing becomes a forgone conclusion, an afterthought.

He heads slowly into the harbor, noticing the emerging detail of every dock and each boat in the first 6 a.m. light. He notices his own boat, too, but feels entwined with it and not separate from it. His body has adapted to it, and his mind to the ocean. Paddling the yellow Tofino is as unconscious an act as making his heart beat. He aims for an empty patch of sand at the base of one of the beacons. With no welcome party in sight, he's content to make land on a neutral beach, land belonging to no one.

And then his bow hits, making that soft sandpaper scrunch he's heard a thousand times. Just like any other landing. But there's no victory elation. No great catharsis. He's already processed the emotion, grappled and silenced needs for a final goal. Gillet just sits in his kayak for long minutes, feeling the firm sand aside his cockpit. He surrenders to the reality that there is no more reason to paddle. No more need to be a part of the boat.

This is it. The trip is over.

CHAPTER TEN
Reentry

33° 0' 44.21" North, 117° 16' 52.60" West—
Cardiff, California
November 2015

"The story would be better if I were dead."

Ed Gillet makes the statement without pause or grin. It's a factual statement from a man very much alive, twenty-eight years removed from the crossing, age sixty-four. He's just making a casual observation, gazing out onto the Pacific from the solid perch of a seaside restaurant deck and looking back with some objective distance at a defined peak of intensity in his life.

He can't help it. Martyrdom would be an impactful closer for the guy who now spends his days teaching narrative structure. In AP literature and AP language-composition courses, the works that Gillet has his students digest are filled with wild survival lessons that only nature can teach man: *Grizzly Years, Into the Wild, The Things They Carried, Heart of Darkness*. The themes get at acceptable risk, what is crazy, the search for truth, the desire to simplify existence.

It's all the same notes. He's just striking them now.

Maybe Gillet's students don't really get the connection between the heady themes and the lived experiences of the man highlighting them— the one who occasionally rides to the large public San Diego–area high school on a motorcycle, whose frizzled shock of red hair is now a shorter more subdued brown, flecked with a little gray.

Every once in a while, an online search leads a student to make the connection. When the student asks about the Hawaii crossing, he simply points them to a YouTube clip—a recording from his appearance on *The Tonight Show*.

"It really says it all," he notes.

In the clip, we see a confident man actualized in full, sharply firing back quips to Johnny Carson.

It's a far cry from the version of Gillet that emerged on the beach August 27, 1987, in Kahului Harbor. Or, more accurately, attempted to emerge.

After forty nonstop hours spent paddling to the finish, Gillet realized he could not stand on his scarred and atrophied legs. Through pins and needles he propped himself from cockpit to sand. As he pushed himself up and worked to straighten his knees, he could only lurch from side to side. As the motion returned and he hobbled forward, he still couldn't pick up his left foot, so he just dragged it, "like Igor following Dracula."

His first human contact was a lone drunk, who teetered toward him in the waking hours, thinking he'd perhaps found a kindred spirit. Gillet asked him for a hand dragging his boat farther up the beach, revealing how he had just paddled over from California, to which the derelict stranger responded, "Two months in dat little thing?"

Gillet grew anxious, curious about what could have happened to his welcoming party. Perhaps they got the last Argos satellite transmission as he was still far offshore, assuming his landing approach would be to Hana on the island's east side.

And what about that McDonald's?

To find out if there were any Golden Arches toasting multiple McMuffins in Kahului, Gillet approached a man changing a tire. Before giving him a quick once-over, an authoritative no, and then promptly driving away, Gillet got a good smell of the man. Still in his feral sea state, senses hyper acute, Gillet picked up the man's distinct morning scents of soap and shampoo.

Suddenly more self-aware of his own odors, he lurched back to the kayak to grab a slightly fresher Capilene T-shirt, brush his teeth, and remove his "unspeakably dirty" long-john underwear in favor of the heavier blue-pile pants stowed after his trying first two weeks working his way off the California coast. With no wallet, no credit cards, no ID—must-haves for a tourist haven—Gillet fished out a roll of twenty-five dollar bills and a pair of stowed nylon flip-flops and headed in toward the nearby Maui Beach Hotel.

The lobby clerk met Gillet's crazed eyes. Knowing just how homeless he must have looked, Gillet needed to put the clerk at ease. He calmly spelled it out: "I just want to make a phone call."

Katie Kampe was not interested in another phone call. Each call chipped away at her faith. By Day 64 of the crossing, she had arrived back to the stress of the shop after her kayak pickup run to the Bay Area. She needed to get away from the calls and the questions and the echoes of uncertainty. She knew he was OK, but she also knew that he must be out of food, and suffering for it. She needed to clear her mind. She did what Ed would: headed to sea. Katie rowed her single shell alone past the Mission Bay jetty. Out to the blue expanse. She looked west and said, "OK, Ed, I've had enough. It's time to get in."

Katie returned to the shop where Alex was running things for the day. When she swung her van back behind the storefront, the VW bus's distinctive rumble alerted Alex, who came bounding out the back door.

"He came running down and he grabs me and I thought, 'What the hell are you doing?'" Kampe recalled. "He says, 'He's alive,' and he picks me up, he's this giant Dutch guy, and he starts twirling me: 'Aliiiiive!'" Still confused, Kampe pushed him off. "'He's alive?' I ask, and he says, 'Ed!'"

Gillet had a nearly identical experience. Alex had picked up the phone ringing from the line at the Maui Hotel. Upon hearing Ed's voice, all he said was, "Fuck, you're alive!"

"What do you mean 'I'm alive?'" Gillet questioned. "Was there any doubt?"

Before Alex could answer, Gillet had another question: "Didn't you know I'd be landing on Maui today?"

"No, we had no idea," Oppedyk answered. "That satellite thing hasn't worked in quite a while."

The weight of the broken Argos unit began to sink in. Gillet pictured the ripple effects of the stress and strain that the device's failure might have caused loved ones. After hearing that Katie was out rowing on the water, he cut things off with Alex and immediately phoned his father.

His father picked up fast, and with the prompt to accept the collect-call charges, immediately talked over the operator.

"Stand aside and let my son talk," Gillet Sr. said.

"Dad, I'm here safe and by God I made it!" Gillet said. He then apologized for running late, explaining the calm seas, the inability to launch the kite and hold a high-mileage pace.

"I thought you wouldn't make it this time," Ed Gillet Sr. told his son, catching him up to speed on his attempts to call in a rescue, and how he would immediately alert the Coast Guard on his safe arrival accordingly.

The thought of a search on his behalf provided an uneasy gaze at the strange bigger picture. He narrowed his view back to the present. It was 9 a.m., and there he was, lurched over next to the lobby pay phone, gripping it with both hands for stability on his shaky legs. He gave his dad the number listed on the top of the phone and headed back to the place he knew and understood. He returned to the kayak.

First, however, he needed a quick pit stop at the gift shop commissary, where he headed straight for the ice cream freezer. Looking over the goods, he realized this wouldn't be quick. He hobbled back and forth from the goodie racks to the counter, creating a small pile: pint of Häagen-Dazs, cookies, candy bar, M&Ms, potato chips, the triangular box of dried-up ham sandwich, quart of milk, and a Coke. The cashier eyed the pile, then eyed Gillet, looking "like a bum who had slept too close to the sprinklers."

"Where you been?" she asked as Gillet filled up a coffee, eyeing the latest issue of *Time*—Steve Martin hamming on the cover, with a feature on "America's Ghettos."

"Uhh, out fishing," he said as he added the magazine to the pile.

Walking better with his twenty-two dollars of calories, Gillet parked it in the shade of a palm tree. Sitting with the cool grass on his skin, on the solid earth, he looked out at the Pacific, noticing the whitecaps in the harbor signaling friendly trade winds. He chugged the milk first and then moved on to the ice cream, catching up on the news between bites. That was the moment. It was one that lasted. One he would later recall with clarity as being as "satisfied as I have ever been in my life."

"I had absolutely no desire to be anywhere else or do anything different," he said. "Just sitting there completely at peace."

Maybe the Argos breaking down wasn't such a bad thing. Arriving under the radar made sense. "I'm just thinking, 'Hey, I'm here. This is good.'"

As Gillet Sr. finished with his call to the Coast Guard, he alerted the rest of the family.

"It was like you could exhale after two months," Catherine Gillet said, as the news made its way to other friends. Russ Davis was on an oceanographic cruise in the Gulf of Alaska when a telex message came through. "Honestly," wrote a relieved Davis, "I was never happier anytime in my life!"

Gillet's sense of accomplished peace and hard-earned bliss, sitting there eating ice cream and reading a magazine in the palm shade, did not last. The only force capable of shattering such a deep layer of comfort was the media. The first incursion arrived quietly as Ed Tanji, a Maui-based writer for the *Honolulu Advertiser*, approached Gillet. He had spotted the kayak driving by in his truck and asked if he was the guy who paddled over from the mainland.

Gillet gave a clear account about what happened to Tanji, who noted how matter-of-factly he related what happened. The story checked out; Tanji handed him a copy of the newspaper, with Gillet pictured right there, the thirty-six-year-old man featured in an "overdue at sea" story Tanji had just written. Gillet grabbed the paper and started reading. It mentioned his parents urging President Reagan to mount a search and a quote from the Coast Guard explaining its refusal. The attention brought back the anxiety from the call with his father. Why the attention? Why were news organizations calling him lost?

He needed to talk to Katie. Upon returning to the hotel lobby, the pay phone was ringing. Tanji followed Gillet, corralling some bellhops and hotel staffers to grab the kayak, and alerting the front desk to let him use their phone.

When the call to the shop picked up, it sounded crazy. "Noises of a party starting," Gillet recalled. "Friends and customers coming by to celebrate and offer congratulations."

When he finally got Kampe on the line, she didn't ask him much.

"I didn't need to know anything," she said. "I just needed to know where he was." She assured him, through all the commotion, that she would be there soon.

She told him how they'd raised enough money through the shop sweepstakes—win a piece of gear from Gillet's trip by guessing his arrival date—as well as a couple friends offering to help, that they could afford to fly the kayak back too.

Thinking of loading the kayak up into a plane, Gillet fired back a knee-jerk response. "Let's paddle around the islands!" he said, considering all the effort to get the tandem boat there.

Kampe hung up and called to book the flight. Ready to be gone, away from the weeks of conjecture about her husband's fate, and away from increasing calls from reporters looking for a quote to tie together their pieces on Gillet's "back-from-the-dead" arrival. "I was already a bit hostile that they said he was dead," Kampe said of the media inquiries. "I answered a few questions but they were pointless—Ed was there, he'd done it."

Gillet hung up the desk phone and moved to the pay phone. His sister called the number that her father had given her. She was still crying with relief. "He just seemed very much like himself," she said. "In a dry, nonplussed sort of way he just said, 'Yeah, I made it. Yep, over sixty-three days, ate my toothpaste.'"

The pay phone kept ringing. Newspaper reporters on one call, magazine writers on the next. The barrage of questions began to wear Gillet down. Quite literally, as the conversations wore on—trying to explain his intentions, describe his reason, extrapolate what might come next—Gillet began growing woozy with all the talking, slouching down on the ground next to his bag of junk food.

One of the big Samoan staffers who helped pull his kayak up onto the hotel lawn, propped Gillet up and helped him into a hotel room. The straight lines and tight walls of the hall were one thing, but the most disorienting factor awaited him in the room: the mirror. When Gillet looked into his eyes, he was shocked at the gaunt figure looking back. Cheeks hollowed, face burnt, frame pared to muscle and bone with nearly forty pounds shed off, body covered in sores, hands "like cooked lobster claws."

The warm shower water at first refreshed his spirits, but the novelty slowly turned. Each minute washed away a little more of all the work to harden himself. The reentry to the ordinary had begun. "I knew it might be a long time before I could return to a life lived at that level of intensity."

Sleep was impossible. The bed was still rocking, yawing against the sea anchors. The silence, deafening. His senses were still attuned "to the ever present, loud background noises of the wind, waves, and seawater rushing past my kayak hull." His mind now struggled to process the sanitized hotel chatter amplified to unnaturally loud levels: footsteps passing, a door slamming, toilets flushing. The noises jarred and the recirculated air stifled. He jumped to throw back the blinds and open all the windows.

Anxious to see his wife, Gillet returned to the gift shop for a new cotton T-shirt. Still restless, he headed to the airport to wait for her late-arriving evening flight, calculating how, after taking two months to make the crossing from California, she would land a mere fourteen hours after him.

As her plane touched down, Gillet stood waiting impatiently for the stair ramp to wheel out on the tarmac. When he saw Kampe emerge from the plane, he couldn't take it and charged the ramp, forcing a security guard to hold him back.

"I knew you'd make it, Mr. Ed," Katie said through tears.

"I'm sorry for being late," he said back.

When they returned to the hotel room, four quarts of Häagen-Dazs packed in dry ice were waiting. (Word had spread about his cravings.) They stayed up eating the well-wishers' ice cream and talking about the crossing, catching up on all that happened at the shop while Ed was away.

"I just needed to know that he was alive and that we were together," Kampe said.

After finally nodding off around 5 a.m., the room phone began ringing with media requests. One of the early morning calls was from Jim McCawley, a producer with *The Tonight Show*, who invited Gillet to appear on the program. They'd have to be at the Burbank studio in five days, and NBC would foot the bill for the plane tickets. Gillet longed to stay on the islands and tour with Kampe in the Tofino, but McCawley upped his offer to where the cash-strapped couple couldn't refuse: They would also cover the freight charges for the kayak.

Gillet accepted the offer, and then unplugged the phone to sleep until the breakfast buffet opened.

Upon waking, he opened the door onto a pile of flower leis, bottles of champagne, and congratulatory telegrams from friends. Kampe noticed her husband was still struggling to walk and offered a hand, though Gillet refused. Trip after trip to the breakfast buffet, Gillet powered through two straight hours of syrupy calorie consumption. Alarmed at his burned hands, sore-covered skin, and atrophied condition, Kampe estimated he had lost up to eighty pounds, nearly twice the amount of weight he claimed. "He was just skin and bones," she said, "like a chemo cancer patient."

He kept filling the bottomless hole of his appetite on the Delta flight back to California. Finally, he got to rip the foil off the box of pineapple chicken and taste that wilted salad. Each bite of the mushy carrot cake finale was the realization of so many empty fantasies roiled inside the dark, soggy confines of that fiberglass shell.

Asking the flight attendant for a second meal, he explained how he was the kayaker mentioned in that morning's newspaper. Instead of yielding a second sympathy meal, however, the request backfired by only alerting other passengers. A native Hawaiian helped subdue Gillet's rising levels of self-consciousness after approaching Gillet just to shake his hand. He wanted to just tell him "thanks for the proof, brah." His journey helped validate long-held beliefs. Hawaiian legends, he told Gillet, connected their homeland to the mainland, where his native ancestors sailed west from North America, likely around British Columbia, tracing the same route along prevailing trades to the islands. The pleasure from the praise didn't last. Gillet slumped back into his seat as he stared down toward the distant ocean, feeling more separate from it and increasingly more like the rest of the load of ordinary well-fed tourists returning to regular lives, "happy and unfulfilled; despairing and satisfied."

When Gillet strode out onto *The Tonight Show* stage, he still looked the part of a tourist, emerging from the curtains in a festive blue Hawaiian shirt. The well-fed part, not so much. Though six days removed from his landing, Gillet cleaned up well. Toasted lobster mitts on the mend, Gillet's belt—down from size 34 to 30—cinched his shirt tucked into khakis hanging loose on his scrawny frame as he walked out to Doc Severinsen's rendition of *Row, Row, Row Your Boat.*

Normally, this kind of nationally broadcast attention might spike Gillet's nerves, such a powerfully amplified version of the simple recognition on the flight. But returning from such vast surroundings into the "small and tawdry" innards of the TV studio put the stakes in perspective.

He walked into the spotlight "calm and detached," confidently leaping up onto the stage to greet Carson and Ed McMahon as the September 2 show's first marquee guest.

When he first sat in the chair, he reeled back a bit from Carson's first question—"What possessed you?"—providing frank and simple wide-eyed responses:

"It was as hard a trip as I thought I could do successfully," Gillet said, citing his knowledge of the winds and current. "It takes the right kayak: had to be big enough to carry all my gear, small enough for me to push."

"So, it's never been done before?" Carson followed.

To that, Gillet recoiled a bit again, providing an instant correction.

"Well, the Hawaiians got there by canoes," he said.

As he went on to explain his experience, cataloging the basics of the trip from a removed distance—his desire to get offshore, the failure of the beacon, navigating by sextant, the winds dying, legs atrophying, living off backpacking food and desalinated water—Gillet gets more comfortable. Noting his fear of missing the islands and drifting to Japan, he looks up, suddenly aware of the audience's aahs and uncomfortable laughter.

To a question of getting scared, Gillet even mentioned the will he composed, ultimately adopting "the philosophy of Scarlett O'Hara: Tomorrow is another day; I'll wait and see."

Following a commercial break, Gillet's comfort in the hot seat only increased as he began to go tit-for-tat with Carson, having a little more fun as they ran through a handful of blown-up photos developed from Gillet's Nikonos reel of 35mm film.

"That was my pet mahi, a fish that traveled with me," Gillet deadpanned, "I ate him eventually." To quiet the erupting laughter, Carson could only play the crowd by saying, "Look folks, it's a cruel world. It's not like a dog, it doesn't get your slippers."

After the show-and-tell, Carson and Gillet headed down to the stage typically reserved for musical acts. For Gillet, standing next to his familiar kayak, propped up on sawhorses, felt like "visiting with an old friend." Gillet's comfort only increased as he ran through the bilge system and bulkheads.

"It's like the *Titanic*," he mugged. "It can never sink."

As Carson rounded out the interview segment, he asked if Gillet would ever do it again, to which Ed replied no, his Hawaii trip was "once in a lifetime."

With all said and done, episode wrapped, standing outside the studio with Kampe, Gillet felt like he had been "transported into the belly of an alien spacecraft, probed and examined for a few hours, and dumped in a Kansas cornfield."

The fallout from the appearance was immediate. Back in San Diego, on his first bike ride into the shop, drivers who spotted the new local celebrity called out to him. Kayaking in the bay, passersby would jeer, "Hey, you going to Hawaii?"

The recognition was not so welcome. Extra attention for the feat only chafed Gillet's reentry back to life on business hours as a proprietor and guide. The feat that he had accomplished, and the distance that he had crossed was so large that it was hard to frame it in chance conversations so fleeting and small. He needed the time and context to shape it correctly. He hosted some casual slideshows in the parking lot behind the shop. Other kayakers and sailors at least had some ability to grasp the sheer scale of the venture—over nine straight weeks making an average of over thirty-five miles a day to cover the same distance that separates Los Angeles and New York—and to appreciate the costs. It was tougher and much more frustrating to detail his experiences with those not oriented to the ocean or keen on outdoor endurance activities.

Even at presentations with like-minded adventurers fluent in risk, something was lost in his attempts to translate. To the self-reliant, he did not need to justify underlying motivations, but was forced to defend his actions and preparation. At a local climbing store, Gillet walked a small crowd though the rudder-breakdown episode and his decision making upon installing the backup. Kampe still remembers the late San Diego climbing icon Werner Landry interjecting, to some laughter, that had Gillet paddled back in to safety, "We would've cut off his balls!"

"It's too easy to say what somebody should have done," Kampe says. "The overwhelming feeling was that people just didn't understand."

For Kampe, understanding came from the inner circle of sea kayaking acquaintances who also had weathered expeditions together. A letter from Bea Dowd, the wife of Kampe's then-business partner, John, struck the only resonant notes in acknowledging her side of journey. "Right now, you're the one I'd like to congratulate," she wrote Katie, "for feeling your way through all this with so much grace and strength and intelligence. It was one big crossing you made, lady." Gillet too gave the committed sea kayaking crowd a final chance, heading up to do a presentation back at the familiar symposium event in Port Townsend, Washington, with all the still-fledging sport's big names in attendance.

At the formal presentation, looking upon the projection of one his photos, Gillet choked up. The exposure to his own desperate outer limit was still unbearably fresh. The images put him right back there, locked in the kayak, straddling the edge of his endurance.

He never invited this kind of public view into his inner life. That question from Carson: Would you do it again? It kept coming up. The mounting list of other casual and misplaced questions, the ones that had no casual answer—Was it fun? How did you go to the bathroom? Where did you land every night?—began to wear. Each incursion rubbed the scar tissue of survival trauma raw once again.

When people asked, he started denying that he was the Hawaii kayaker. He stopped mentioning it to new customers at the shop. He stopped accepting interview requests. It was easier to avoid it altogether.

"I was just too hostile," Gillet said. He went back to the vow of silence that he made in the kayak. Speaking of the feat would only detract power from the test of self.

"It all got swept up," Kampe said. "It was too big for me to deal with. And it was too big for Ed to deal with, so we ignored it and moved on with the business."

To mark the end of their first season in business, they headed to Baja that November 1987—to paddle the Gulf side of the peninsula from San Felipe to La Paz. Gillet also wanted back in his kayak. "My attachment to the kayak was so profound," he said. "And it was a way of getting her to share that experience."

The occasional tours in the Tofino with Kampe were the extent of Gillet's willingness to share mentions of his experience. As San Diego's only specialty sea kayak dealer at the time, Southwest Kayaks' walk-in and referral business continued to grow. For every one of the next fourteen years that they ran the shop together, open 362 days a year, Gillet distanced himself from the summer of 1987. The more that Gillet remained silent, the more the story of his undertaking became loaded with mystery and imbued with intrigue.

And each year that passed, the Hawaii crossing continued to go untouched, unremarked upon in any way. As decades mounted without anything resembling a repeat effort, the feat and the man behind it became the stuff of paddling legend.

Chapter Eleven

The Duplicators

As Gillet remained silent for the next twenty-five years, and with no other paddlers even attempting the crossing again, his stature only grew. In sea kayaking circles, the crossing from Monterey to Hawaii became sacrosanct.

"The most insane hard-core thing that I've ever heard of," is one way to put it. That's how Gillet's accomplishment is viewed by Sean Morley, who has as firm a grasp as any modern expedition sea kayaker on where the Hawaii crossing fits into annals of the sport. Morley has certainly left his mark there, having set both speed crossing and circumnavigation records, including a six-month, forty-five-hundred-mile solo circumnavigation of Ireland plus every inhabited island in his native United Kingdom.

To Morley, a Cornish policeman who reoriented his life and career around the world of sea kayaking—everything from surf competition to sales, events, and instruction—Gillet's expedition stands alone. "The guy is without doubt a living legend," Morley adds. "Essentially it's a tandem sea kayak that he's paddling solo . . . a boat anybody could have purchased. Whereas when you look at the Atlantic [kayak-paddled] crossings, Peter Bray [2001] and Aleksander Doba ['11, '14, and '17]— I'm not taking away from their achievements—but that is a very specialized kayak they've built. So, the fact Gillet is paddling a boat that anybody could have gotten ahold of, that sets it apart."

Other longtime mainstays of the West Coast sea kayaking scene agree. Gillet's crossing left a lasting mark. "We were all blown away by what he was able to endure," Bob Licht says of Gillet. "The idea of pontoons and standing up to do a sextant, I still talk about that with people. Sliding down into cockpit to sleep, having the fish follow him so that's what he ate? I mean come on, it's crazy."

Crazy is relative. And in 2012 an enigmatic American adventurer named Wave Vidmar dusted off the dormant idea of kayaking to Hawaii. Known for his polar treks, Vidmar, at forty-eight, set out to replicate Gillet's solo paddling journey from a practical perspective—by using a reinforced stock tandem kayak, and by also launching from the Bay Area. From a philosophical perspective, however, Vidmar's approach could not have been more different. Vidmar blitzed sponsors and media alike for support and attention.

The high-profile campaign to fund and hype the expedition paid off, landing Vidmar the right equipment and media coverage. The *New York Times* and local news outlets alike thoroughly documented Vidmar's pickup of a stock twenty-two-foot tandem sea kayak from Vancouver Island's Seaward Kayaks. The crew at Seaward customized a sleek white Passat G3, adding an additional twenty pounds of composite matting and Kevlar and carbon-fiber reinforcements to the hull and deck. Vidmar said it was a $10,000 kayak. Local members of the Chemainus First Nations community blessed Vidmar's new 125-pound seafaring craft, adorning it with orca decals. The media outlets framed the Hawaii crossing as the "Mount Everest of Sea Kayaking." Gillet became Sir Edmund Hillary; the expedition a benchmark to repeat, a feat to improve upon.

Vidmar's launch in June, then August, then October, was beset with multiple delays, citing electrical, equipment, and personal issues. By the late fall, days prior to a rescheduled Bay Area launch, he approached the California Canoe & Kayak shop where Morley was then working as the program director. Vidmar was looking for a compass donation.

"I was blown away that by this point, he didn't have a compass," says Morley, skeptical about committing to sponsoring him with gear. Hearing more about Vidmar's setup and plan only triggered other "alarm bells." Like Gillet, he planned to rig sponsors aside his cockpit at night, however, the rigging was through simple plastic padeyes that didn't look up to the task. Vidmar had cut the foot pedals controlling his rudder down to small metal slivers, hoping to create more room to slide into the hull. "It just looked like it would be excruciating," said Morley. "When I've done long trips, it's your feet that get more sore than probably any other part of your body because they are in contact with the foot brakes/pedals all the time." And then there was the impractical late-season launch. "In my opinion," Morley concludes, "he was doomed from the start."

Vidmar eventually departed at the end of a short winter day on Christmas Eve 2012, just north of San Francisco in Bodega Bay—a move that would extend his expedition's mileage a few hundred past Gillet's.

Though Vidmar pushed his launch 150 miles north of Monterey, he still paddled right into the same immediate weather problems as Gillet. After an evening departure, the harrowing onshore conditions turned on during the early morning hours of Vidmar's first day at sea. Tossed in heaving waves for what he reported as fifteen hours, Vidmar signaled his rescue beacon just over twenty-four hours after his launch. The Coast Guard picked him up about fifteen miles offshore. The fancy kayak was not as fortunate.

That night, the Coast Guard attempted to tow Vidmar's loaded kayak back into Bodega Bay. In the stormy conditions, a wave swamped and swallowed the kayak, jarring it loose from the towline. The Christmas Day offering to the sea marked a peculiar end to Vidmar's expedition.

The information on the rescue and the fate of the kayak only came from Seaward, hoping to put some closure on an episode that seemed like a remarkable journey and strategic marketing play for their kayaks. Vidmar turned more reclusive than Gillet. He published no online posts and made no public comments on the episode. When prompted for an interview with *Canoe & Kayak* magazine, he said that he would only speak for a $5,000 fee.

Clay Biles was much more forthcoming. Months after Vidmar's attempt, Biles—another San Francisco Bay Area kayaker—was the next to take a crack at Gillet's crossing. Biles also made no secret of his desire to cover the distance exactly as Gillet had: from the same Monterey launch; at the same age as Gillet; with the same kayak, the Tofino's successor, a twenty-two-foot Necky Nootka Plus tandem. Prior to his intended launch in mid-April 2013, Biles opened up his home to talk through his intentions, and then opened up his garage to a walk-through inspection of the strung-up kayak that he had spent over a year modifying for the journey ahead.

For Biles, then a Federal Air Marshal and father of three, retired from active naval duty in special warfare, the crossing represented "a final bucket list thing," before he could take life a little easier and "go relax in suburbia-land." He carried a no-nonsense attitude and an intense can-do military approach to the trip. The crossing was not an existential search; it was simply "a major endurance test—but anybody is capable of that," he said, framing it more as a task to complete using allotted days off. "I've got a family," he said in even measures, boxes of gear stacked in the garage between kids' toys. "I'm not suicidal. I know I'll get it done."

Though he never actually connected with Gillet, Biles had soaked up every interview and each morsel of information dug up from the few news and interview pieces released following his 1987 journey. Biles followed the word of Gillet like it was the gospel. He took out the seats and center-rear bulkhead to create a six-foot sleeping cavity, just like Gillet. He read an archived online magazine piece about the failed front hood cover, so he sealed his front cockpit shut, affixing a rectangular opening from the retrofitted lid of a waterproof Pelican case. He heard about Gillet's wishes for a rear canopy cover, so he added a dodger that could flip up to cover the rear cockpit. He even heeded a joke Gillet made about wanting to pack extra SPAM into the empty packing spaces of the cockpit, so he stocked up on tins of the gelatinized protein.

Objectively, Biles was equipped for a successful bid. Plus, he added a few technological bells and whistles to stack the deck, including a satellite phone and 12-volt battery with an inverter to power an AIS ship ID system and GPS navigation. But Biles veered from Gillet in a few key areas—the most consequential decision being his choice to paddle with a partner.

R. W. Hand, a friend of Biles from the Federal Air Marshal Service, was also retired from an elite special forces service (the Army Rangers) and looking for an adventure. Hand rigged his own Nootka Plus separately from Biles in the landlocked center of Colorado. Hand, then at age fifty-six, stayed fit by paddling his tandem kayak in reservoirs, hiking, and working as a wildland firefighter, maintaining a daunting physique and white handlebar moustache that could easily have him cast as a body double for Hulk Hogan. The two delayed the initial launch after some work complications for Biles, finally meeting to load out their matching red kayaks in Monterey in early June, six months after Vidmar's aborted attempt. Despite their limited experience with expedition paddling on the open ocean, or with one another on any kind expedition, the pair remained confident. Get separated? "We'll just press on," Biles said. "We can sustain ourselves individually."

The pair seemed like they would make a good team: Hand was the towering, soft-spoken elder wingman deferring the lead to the wiry and restless Biles, a foot shorter and almost two decades younger, at age thirty-seven. However, just eight hours after their June 8, 2013, launch, Biles was back in Monterey, courtesy of a Coast Guard assist, followed by Hand, paddling his kayak back to the harbor.

The plan was to raft their fully loaded sea kayaks together during resting phases. That plan had never been tested, especially not in the punishing offshore conditions that Biles and Hand experienced hours into their bid to get offshore. As a storm hit, Biles deployed his sea anchor so that Hand could tie off. But in the heaving waves and windy conditions, Hand couldn't stop paddling to effectively throw his line, so he had to line up with Biles to tether on. That's when the composite kayaks collided. With Biles's boat taking on water and the integrity of Hand's craft in question, Biles called the Coast Guard.

When the ship arrived, Hand refused a ride in. Though the storm had blown the two kayakers north of Monterey, the Coast Guard deemed Hand capable enough to paddle back into the harbor on his own accord. But after the Coast Guard left with Biles, Hand turned west to Hawaii—back into the storm. Then a "nagging voice" in the back of his head told him otherwise. It wouldn't cost him any time, he figured, to head into Monterey to inspect any damage. And it wasn't until he got into the protected waters and emerged from the boat that he noticed the four-inch gash through the red gel coating of his kayak's bow.

The idea of a "mission undone" gnawed at Hand over the next year. Retired from the Air Marshals in 2012, the father of two typically spent his free time between firefighting stints by riding his motorcycle on windy mountain roads or ticking off all but one of Colorado's fifty-four fourteen thousand–foot peaks. But that summer, all he could think about was where he fell short. He got to fixing the crack in his kayak hull.

"Too many people kind of get in a boring routine: go to work, go home, sit on the couch, watch sports," Hand explained in the slower cadence of his native West Texas drawl. "I told my daughter you just have to go out of your comfort zone to test yourself. It's the only way to learn."

Less than a year later, Hand felt that he'd gleaned enough information to relaunch the expedition solo. On May 30, 2014, he departed again from Monterey Harbor, in the style of Ed Gillet: with no sponsor or media or Coast Guard notifications. Aside from Hand's dropoff/ground support, his friend David White posting a few updates on Hand's personal Facebook profile, there was barely a trace of the expedition.

Lessons learned included a few rigging tweaks. Hand left the rear cockpit dodger behind in favor of a jury-rigged system of tent poles to prop his storm cag (integrated jacket and spraydeck) over him at night. He added two solar panels to charge a pair of GPS devices. He left behind the kite, but kept a simpler version of Gillet's inflatable stabilizers with a pair of white boat fenders he could lash to the sides. He once again packed food for a full sixty days, including a few morale cigars. Finally, he mounted a camouflage Mickey Mouse head with a missing ear to the front deck: a simple reminder of hope for his efforts to somehow raise awareness for a pair of veterans' organizations, the Wounded Warrior Project and the Honor Flight Program.

By Day 2, Hand was paddling right into the toughest conditions that he had ever encountered. From the trough, he estimated looking up thirty feet to the crests of waves—some breaking over him, others breaking on him.

The first capsize "was a learning experience."

While upside down, immersed in the frigid water, he first had to learn to exit the loaded kayak and find his way to the static perimeter line. Then Hand had to pull himself up on the hull, flip the craft, straddle the kayak, and work himself back into the rear cockpit, now submerged underwater while getting pummeled with waves. Finally, he needed to seal the skirt over the cockpit opening, and start pumping out water, all while keeping the kayak pointed into the waves.

Waves that would knock the kayak over again.

After re-flipping and entering his kayak for the second time, Hand also learned the folly of abandoning the full dry suit that he had worn on the first attempt. Instead, he favored a two-piece outerwear setup of separate top and pants. Without a sealed waist, nothing prevented water from rushing inside both the layers. The latex gaskets around his wrists and his ankles, however, prevented water from draining back out. He was soaked, and as he kept paddling into the weather he would steal moments to tug at the gaskets and drain the water—already feeling open sores from rubber stretching at skin.

When the waves flipped Hand for the fourth time, he got tangled in the safety line tethered from around his waist to the kayak. Already exhausted, he wrestled underwater to unwrap the line, down to his "last two seconds of breath." As his air ran out, he untangled the line and came up gasping. He bobbed next to the kayak, vowing never to wear the line again.

"It was a close one," Hand said.

When the waves let up for a spell on Sunday, Hand did an inventory to see that nothing was lost save a pair of sunglasses, which he didn't need in the overcast haze anyway.

"Wet and hungry but having a good time," he sent as an outbound message on Monday to White on his two-way satellite communicator/ GPS device.

The A-OK message understated Hand's dangerous levels of fatigue. "Everything you do out there," Hand said, "from making water to putting the sea anchor out, to retrieving the sea anchor, to trying to stay on course—everything—is just exhausting."

Once the clouds darkened and dusk approached, sleep was not an option. Without a light, paddling without direction was not an option. So, Hand just set his sea anchor, bilged his cockpit, re-lashed his load and hunkered down, crossing his fingers that the roar of the waves would miss him, or at least not break on top of him again.

"If I heard that roar coming all I could do was brace myself and wait for impact," he said. "It was like dumping tons of ice-cold water from a dump truck on you.

"I would just hope that it wouldn't collapse my kayak," he said. "The force was so strong I thought it was gonna break my kayak but it never did. That went on every night I was out there."

Not that Hand could have slept comfortably in calm conditions. He could not even lay down. He was a few inches taller than the six-foot rear cavity inside the cockpit, so he was unable to squeeze his shoulders and head inside the hull even if he tried. He nodded off for catnaps sitting upright like a soldier spiked out in the rain, "shut-eye here and there when I could."

The storms continued through Day 6, when Hand sent a position—35 degrees north and 122 degrees west—roughly eighty miles off the California coast. He has starting to have problems with his navigation system. Maybe he snagged the wire taped underneath the deck—running through the front bulkhead to a 35-amp scooter battery stowed in a cooler in the kayak's middle storage compartment—during one of the flips. Then the battery-powered GPS "just pooped out." The battery system was no longer functional and the deck-mounted, solar-charging system was useless to charge it. Much of the screen on his two-way device was shrouded in condensation with a button damaged. Still, on Day 9, it was functional enough to send the following cryptic message out to White: "Thnking abot heabing to la need to see if solar can be fbxed."

After nine days of taking "a beating every day," Hand made his decision. It was the same day that Gillet had, at first, chosen to turn back for the coast following his rudder damage. Hand spent the next three days and two nights paddling straight, with no sleep in busy waters.

And then, just like Gillet, he had a coming to terms as the weather broke in his favor. "I spent two or three hours saying, 'Do I want to go east or west?'" Hand recalled. "I'd paddle west a while and say, 'Dad-gummit, I should go in while I'm so close to land, fix whatever broke the solar system,' then I turned around and couldn't decide—back and forth, back and forth."

Hand had no idea that after the last message, White had called the Coast Guard and alerted them to his friend's position about eighty-five miles off the California coast, as well as his equipment-failure circumstances. And after hearing the Coast Guard's forecast of a large storm system on the way, White made the rescue call.

When he spotted the helicopter, Hand was enjoying some much-needed sunshine on his twelfth day out, unaware the fair weather was just the calm before the storm. He was also unaware that, despite his heading east toward the coast, he was still drifting farther out to sea.

"I thought it was just a routine patrol and they wouldn't go away," Hand laughs. "Finally, they got a radio down to me and I paddled over and they said, 'We've got a ship coming to you in a couple hours.' I told them, 'Don't. I don't need a rescue!'"

Hand kept paddling as the helicopter circled. Finally, when the rigid inflatable launch boat arrived, Hand swallowed his pride, accepted the rescue, and rationalized accepting assistance in knowing that they were all "going in anyway."

What Hand could not accept was the way that the rescue crew transferred his kayak from sea level up to the deck of the 225-foot USCGC *Aspen*. The crew opted to use a cargo net, but when the heavily loaded and waterlogged kayak slipped out, the only hauling option left was hoisting it straight up the side of the ship by the sea-anchor line attached to the bow. Hand cringed as the cutter's crew heaved the dangling fiberglass tube up, and then folded it with a crunch over the fulcrum edge of the ship to pull it aboard.

Once again, Hand was headed back home to Colorado. Though he suffered no injuries, the thought of a mission undone still burned inside.

"It's a doable thing," Hand said resolutely, looking back on his twelve days at sea. "I just picked the wrong year." He didn't have much else to say. After two weeks back on land, Hand posted a spartan message on Facebook: "California to Hawaii 2015."

Once unloaded and dried out, however, he was looking at more than a four-inch gash on his kayak. He needed a lot more fiberglass and epoxy for the significant cracks along both seams and on both deck and hull where the loaded kayak flexed and partially snapped over the ship's edge. So, over the winter, he patched and glued. He reinforced. He backed up electronics. He thought about mistakes and failures. He ditched the dry wear for some neoprene, military-issue base layers. "I had it down to a science," Hand said.

The analytical forethought cut out one factor entirely: no more time wasted in the harbor. Hand knew that he had burned way too much daylight and energy on prior attempts hemming and hawing over his gear pile, moving items from truck to kayak, stuffing and loading instead of making immediate miles. He rented a trailer and loaded up his (re)reinforced red Nootka Plus. That April, Hand backed his loaded vessel down the launch ramp and slipped out of Monterey Harbor "as smooth as silk" for the most silent attempt at the Pacific kayak crossing to date.

As the tide was going out, the sun was coming up, and Hand, paddling "on a natural high," was on his way to Hawaii.

Right before he left the protection of the harbor, he noticed a little water in the cockpit. "Dad-gummit," Hand said, thinking it was residual water from the launch. "I couldn't believe it, didn't want to believe it."

Ocean currents immediately swept Hand south, as the internal water level kept rising, seeping through the patches. By the time he began bailing, Hand realized his third bid was over. He paddled all night against the current, arriving back in the harbor, defeated once again, after thirty-seven nonstop hours. There's no way to back up a compromised hull.

Hand realizes the irony of being landlocked in the arid foothills of southern-central Colorado, riding his Harley, climbing mountains, fighting wildland fires, all the while thinking and dreaming of the empty canvas of the open ocean.

"Never in my wildest dreams would I have imagined kayaking to Hawaii until Clay got me into doing it," Hand says, "and now it's like an obsession."

"It's something I have got to do," Hand added, trying to explain the itch. "A monkey on my back. I've just got to do it and get it over with."

If only, Hand seems to think, he had the right kayak. However, now the once venerable Necky Kayaks is no more—bought by Johnson Outdoors (of the Johnson & Johnson corporate family) and discontinued in favor of more intermediate recreational offerings under other labels in its brand portfolio. Hand was left on the hunt for a new seaworthy stock offering: big enough for the gear and his lumbering frame, small enough to paddle efficiently. In the summer of 2017, he made the drive from Colorado to Vancouver Island to pick up an even larger tandem option from Atlantis Kayaks. Hand then spent the winter wiring a solar panel system and prepping the massive ninety-six-pound Synergy Safari model, complete with a custom paint job: red, white, and blue deck; white hull marked by irregular black stripes stacked along the 22.5-foot length, designed like an enlarged UPC code to confuse and deter sharks. Though it has a Kevlar-reinforced bow with a twin keel for added stability, at the time of press, Hand had yet to paddle it on the open ocean prior to his projected late-spring launch back at Monterey Harbor. Attempt Number

Four. "Hope it isn't too hard to maneuver in big waves because of its size," he wrote.

The boat is simply a means to an end. A way to complete unfinished business. It's less of an open-ended inquiry into personal limits, as it was for Gillet, than it was and it is a need to measure up to self-imposed expectations. It's about integrity. Being a man of his word. Peace of mind, knowing that the itch of the unrelenting Pacific is finally scratched. As Hand put it: "I think about it all the time."

CHAPTER TWELVE

The Pioneers

R. W. HAND WAS NOT THE FIRST MODERN PADDLER TO LOSE SLEEP OVER the open challenge of the Pacific, ultimately lured to its siren call. Neither was Gillet.

That would be James Brinton, whose original attempt at a solo, human-powered crossing ended in tragedy. Brinton was a Seattle college student who set off in 1971 for a three-month journey from La Push, Washington, to Japan. Twenty-four hours after Brinton launched the seven thousand–mile expedition from the western edge of the Olympic Peninsula, a fisherman spotted his kayak four miles offshore. In eight-foot seas and twenty-five-knot winds, the bobbing fourteen-foot kayak was capsized, and empty.

Despite a Coast Guard search with two aircraft and one cutter, Brinton was never found. His stepfather, James Moore, was surprised, knowing that Brinton, at age twenty-five, was a strong swimmer and likely wearing his life jacket and wet suit. An Eagle Scout at fifteen, and an accomplished sailor who ventured through the Baltic to the North Sea at sixteen, with a tour of duty in Vietnam under his belt, Brinton had returned home to the Pacific Northwest, studying to be a teacher. Friends reported that Brinton had been eating raw fish for months, preparing for the hardships of the journey with five-mile training swims in Puget Sound, all winter, with no wet suit.

Still, Moore was curious why Brinton had not spent more time paddling his kayak in different conditions, especially with the full load of three hundred pounds. In the Associated Press account of the unsuccessful search, the only way that Moore could rationalize his stepson's journey was as an obsession.

"There was nothing anyone could do to stop him," Moore said. "Jim always loved the water, but he just got possessed with an idea, and once he got it, that was it."

Marilyn Tubbs covered Brinton's "morbid sendoff" from the La Push marina docks for the *Port Angeles Evening News* on the afternoon of June 12, 1971. Tubbs cataloged Brinton's preparedness for the challenges ahead—with a freshwater distillation system, fishing gear, rationed and well-thought-out provisions vetted by expert dietitians, a powerful radio, a radar deflector to avoid ships, and even plans to connect with a Canadian weather vessel.

Before climbing in the overloaded kayak, Brinton spent over an hour silently walking the beach. After long contemplation, he made a decisive exit, a bystander from the docks saying, "We'll be hearing from you from Japan."

Brinton confidently answered, "You better believe it," before paddling away.

Later that summer, on August 21, 1971, Geordie Tocher crashed his handcrafted sailing canoe into the rocky reefs outside of Bodega Bay, California. The mishap in the fog put an abrupt end to nineteen days spent working his way out to the Pacific from West Vancouver, British Columbia, around the tip of the Olympic Peninsula, past where Brinton had been lost, and along the Northern California coast. Tocher was tracing a path of currents and winds known in native Haida lore to eventually lead south, down away from the continent, and then west—straight to the Hawaiian Islands. He was out to prove the westward mainland-to-island human migration theory popularized by Thor Heyerdahl, albeit with a colorful Scottish Canadian bent.

Tocher embodied the B.C. frontier spirit, with a charismatic, larger-than-life personality, and a six-foot, 225-pound frame to match. Working as a tree faller from age thirteen, Tocher spent over two years hand-carving a two hundred-foot cedar tree into a fifty-two-foot dugout named *Orenda* with a smaller replica lashed to the side to act as a stabilizing outrigger. The jagged reef structure ended those years of labor, but the project had already planted seeds of an idea that set firm roots of possibility in his mind.

Tocher recommitted to the crossing. He began selling off all his possessions to finance the next journey, which began when Tocher, back in the B.C. woods, spotted an ancient Douglas fir that had been inching skyward like a rod, all three hundred feet straight up over the last seven hundred years. With the eighteen-ton log, Tocher began chiseling away at his next ocean-voyaging craft, *Orenda II*.

Patrick Quesnel had never heard of Tocher. When Quesnel, on the Pacific Northwest's alternate US side of the Canadian border, heard the open call of the Pacific, he thought he was the first to answer that sort of exploratory challenge. He looked back in admiration to 1896, when George Harbo and Frank Samuelsen famously rowed across the Atlantic from New York to Great Britain.

Sure, Quesnel had read *Kon-Tiki*. He knew the migration theories. And growing up in Puget Sound, he had been rowing boats since he could swim a half mile, at age five. By the time he was working his way through the University of Washington, he had no idea what he wanted to do with his life. So, he decided to drop out until he figured it out. He tried a few jobs.

All he knew was that he wanted adventure: "Chopping through the jungles of the Amazon, climbing mountains, canoeing, and all the rest of it," Quesnel recalled. "I found that I still had some of those childhood dreams at twenty, twenty-one, so I thought, 'I ought to do something. The time is now—do it and get it out of your system.'"

"It" was a sailboat. A tour of the South Pacific would be the perfect adventure, Quesnel figured. Then he started doing the math. The number of years it would take on commercial fishing wages to finance a comfortable sailboat was seven too many. He went back to Harbo and Samuelson, the hardy Norwegian Americans whose ocean-crossing mark went unmatched for 114 years. The simplicity of the oars, the timeless design of a dory. He began studying sailing logs, pilot charts of the Pacific. He plotted his route west to Hawaii.

"Finally," he says, "I couldn't think of a good reason not to."

With a set of plans for a basic twenty-one-foot Cape Cod dory—seaworthy, able to hold weight, with minimum power needed for propulsion—Quesnel fixed plywood planks to an Alaskan-cedar frame. That was about the only framework he had. In 1972 few accounts existed of successful open-ocean crossings. There was no relevant information to be gleaned from any library.

"I had to find out by trial and error," Quesnel said. "It's akin to hopping into a car never having driven before, but figuring out how everything works and taking off."

The trial-and-error process began with Quesnel's choice of rowing partners. His pick for his first attempt was not tough enough.

"We didn't have the fantastic gear, "Quesnel said. "We were just cold and wet and our teeth chattered 'til our jaws got numb. It was a tough-it-out thing and he couldn't take the physical hardship and went cold and sleepless." So Quesnel looked for a tougher partner. He picked out "a six-foot-four, ex-Marine barroom brawler" for his second attempt in 1972.

But Quesnel found out quickly that physical toughness wasn't exactly what he needed. During the first storm on the second attempt, his barroom-brawling partner "went to pieces."

He would start screaming before every wave curled over, "babbling about how he was going to join his mother," who it turned out he had lost at an early age. Quesnel worried about what potentially unsafe directions the emotion might lead to. He corralled the knives and hatchets and stuck them in the compartment he sat on. When the storm passed, Quesnel offered him an out, pointed the boat east to shore, and his partner "whipped the water to a froth getting back in."

What Quesnel needed was a partner with "emotional toughness." He found it in "a thirty-five-year-old truck driver who was used to hardship." Despite a late departure with the onset of winter for Quesnel's third attempt in 1972, the pair worked well together through the immediately trying conditions. Then six days in, the partner got a painful kidney infection. Not wanting to take chances, they called in an SOS. Once the Coast Guard picked up his partner, Quesnel had a choice: head back, or continue the crossing alone.

"I figured the loneliness couldn't be any worse than the luck I'd been having with my partners," he said. As the cold and wet days dragged on, and Quesnel made it through the worst three hundred miles, he started to understand the challenge of the solo endeavor.

"It's a benevolent kind of solitude," Quesnel said. "If you are already on the edge to begin with, it could push you over. . . . You have to have a kind of stoic, good ol' Scandinavian type personality. It hurts to have an overactive imagination."

So Quesnel kept his imagination at bay and kept at the task of pulling his boat south until the West Coast receded to the east. About four hundred miles off Baja California, near Ed Gillet's "30-130 target," Quesnel started picking up the northeasterly trade winds. Then after dropping a few more degrees of latitude, he picked up more favorable easterly trades. When he'd see a freighter, he would fire off a flare to flag them down. He would row into the lee of the ship and toss a four-ounce fishing weight lashed via shoestring to a Ziploc bag that held a note. It explained his route with a request to report his position and disposition—healthy and in good spirits—to the Coast Guard.

After three months, with over half of the twenty-seven-hundred miles of his long south- and west-arcing route from Washington to Hawaii completed, Quesnel flagged down a US tanker after thirty-eight days with no contact. In the dark forty-five-knot winds, the tanker mis-timed its approach alongside Quesnel. He disappeared from the ship's aft spotlight, lost in the shadow of the ship's bow. Bearing down on him at about eight knots in the rolling seas, the tanker's bow plunged down onto Quesnel's dory.

"I figured the bow would have to cut through all the wood on the side," said Quesnel, who sprang to the floor, holding onto his seat. Somehow the impact didn't roll his boat, though it tilted the dory up 180 degrees, dumping the contents of the cockpit, filling it with water as it skittered alongside the side of the ship. Quesnel hopped back in to the seat "to row like crazy" to avoid getting sucked into the ship's propeller.

Once the ship had moved back into the darkness, Quesnel's adrenaline levels dropped. He started shaking. That's when he noticed the rudder. Damaged beyond repair, without a spare, Quesnel weighed his options for continuing with the trade winds. After four frustrated hours spent rowing through the night, a freak wave did what the tanker could not, rolling and tossing him from the dory. When the boat righted itself, Quesnel climbed back aboard to find a swamped boat with his sextant missing.

The sextant was the deal breaker. Quesnel armed his SOS bush plane beacon, which was picked up by the Coast Guard's Ocean Station November, then located in the mid-Pacific to aid downed planes headed to Hawaii. In five hours, he was safely on a ship headed home.

Quesnel's resolve was far from broken. He fixed up the same trusty red dory, which he named *Hawaiiki*. He then took a methodical approach to lessons learned through his trio of trials at sea. "I came up with a list of every single reason the first series of attempts failed and one by one went through each thing," Quesnel said. "The number one thing was to go by myself—it was the only way I could guarantee that I'd make it."

As Quesnel went through his checklist in Vaughn, Washington, and Tocher hollowed his massive Doug fir log outside of Vancouver, a navy pilot named Lt. George Sigler was going around to Bay Area marine shops, researching, pricing, and assembling a new survival kit.

Sigler knew that there was only one true way to test, and effectively market, his SIG II Ocean Survival Package. In 1974 he recruited a fellow pilot, Lt. Charlie Gore, to join him in a 15.5-foot Zodiac Mark III inflatable raft for a test voyage. Towed twenty miles outside the Golden Gate, the pair cast themselves adrift on July 4. The plan was to spell each other while taking turns sailing the raft, manning the five-by-seven tarp rigged on a single mast, and ruddering while living off the kit contents that Sigler had acquired—six pounds of candy and vitamins for calorie intake and two solar stills for drinking water. After fifty-five "days of boredom filled with hours of terror," the navy ordered the atrophied guinea pigs (Gore lost nearly sixty pounds) picked up 128 miles off Hawaii.

The trip nearly ended on Day 2 when heavy seas folded the raft in half, violently flipping it and causing the crew to lose its backup equipment.

Quesnel's return bid at the oars, launching again from La Push, Washington, July 14, 1976, also turned into a survival test. Sleeping two hours at a time, biting cardboard to keep his teeth from chattering, his previous attempts had taught him to hang in there in a storm, rowing against the prevailing weather as long as possible before throwing out the sea anchor and being forced to go with it.

Quesnel had passed the halfway point to Hawaii—again—when he was slammed with gale-force tailwinds for two days. He was making good progress by moonlight, rowing at night as he normally did (to rest and be better visible to passing ships by day). But after two straight nights weaving through thirty-foot waves, and two sleepless days at sea anchor getting drenched in his cockpit under wool horse blankets, he needed rest. But the winds would not cooperate. Instead of laying down after a couple of days, like the previous storms, they only increased.

He lost the strength to tighten the canvas storm cover to snap-seal his cockpit. Exhausted and bailing with a five-gallon bucket, Quesnel started hallucinating. Every twenty minutes a breaker over the top would fill the boat again. He'd down a spoonful of instant coffee to help will his body to bail. His muscles weren't working. He sat down to pump the water out with his bilge pump. Looking down, he noticed the bilge pump handle had fallen off. He woke up with his face in water, realizing he had just blacked out.

"Very calmly and dispassionately, I thought, 'I guess this is it,'" Quesnel said. Thinking he'd want whoever found his boat "to find the body" he lashed himself upright in the sitting position, with his head above the waterline of the cockpit. If the next wave filled the boat, his slumped head would be clear.

The next thing Quesnel remembers was the boat sitting still, the wood creaking him awake. The sea anchor was hanging straight down. The storm had passed. Quesnel looked at his watch, it was two hours earlier than when he had tied himself in.

Only then did Quesnel realize that he had been drifting in and out of consciousness for twenty-two hours.

"Really makes you stop and think," says Quesnel.

But not for too long. Looking back, Quesnel simply orders the episode as one of six "emergencies" in between "just a bunch of boredom" during the 111 days it took him to successfully reach Hawaii. The routine was rote: He would row for fifty minutes, read for ten. Keep the mind sharp and pass the time—heady books that stick to your thoughts, the New Testament, Hemingway's *Green Hills of Africa*, and *Helter Skelter*, the 1974 true-crime best seller. For fresh water, Quesnel had lined the space between his hull bottom and floor with four hundred pounds worth of twenty-five-gallon foldable Reliant water jugs, filling the cracks with cans of beer. As the days stacked up and that ballast weight lightened, Quesnel started worrying more about the heat and less about the miles.

Having consumed the three books, most of the water jugs, and all eight cases of beer (salt water corroding the cans faster than he could drink them), Quesnel arrived to Oahu without ceremony. Nobody outside family and friends expected him. Nobody knew what to think of the brawny oarsman wearing a bandana holding back long sun-bleached hair to reveal a blond beard kept trim by nervous teeth chomping off the ends in tense moments. Certainly none of the Honolulu sailors out enjoying a calm morning on November 2, 1976, thought the figure rowing past Koko Head, at the southeast tip of the island, had just accomplished a world's-first feat.

And Quesnel didn't flaunt the facts either, despite his stake to a solid claim as the only solo adventurer to have ever reached the islands entirely by human power. But as a broke twenty-seven-year-old, Quesnel at least knew he had a good story to tell. He sold it to the highest bidder, the *National Enquirer*. Once the gag order was lifted, he made a policy that any time he was "interviewed by a young beautiful reporter and she wasn't wearing a wedding ring, I'd ask her out." He ended up marrying the first reporter he asked out, went into a career in commercial fishing, had two daughters, and just retired last year on an Oregon island near the mouth of the Columbia River.

Forty-one years on, Quesnel can still go straight to that furious second straight night in a row, pulling through the storm, as if no time had passed.

"It was pretty haunting and surreal," Quesnel says of the scene unfolding beneath a full moon. "The thirty-foot waves were glittering in the moonlight, menacing and rolling toward you. And I'm trying to figure out a spot where it's not breaking and head to that spot.

"I was pretty keyed up," he said, "but at the same time, it was exhilarating."

The visceral sensations of the sea at night were forever imprinted on Karin Lind's mind as well. Lind, then a thirty-five-year-old anthropology professor at Vancouver's Capilano University, became romantically involved with Geordie Tocher—the eccentric Canadian canoe crafter— as he neared completion of *Orenda II*. Lind accepted Tocher's invitation to join him and Gerhard Kiesel, a fifty-six-year-old local baker with over thirty thousand miles of sailing experience, on their second attempt to reach Hawaii. The new *Orenda* was shorter at forty-two feet to better handle big waves, and featured a maple outrigger lashed with cedar framework, two sailing masts, and canvas spray coverings fore and aft.

Departing Vancouver on May 14, 1978, after challenging conditions through the Strait of Juan de Fuca, the *Orenda II* finally made it out to the blue waters of the Pacific.

On calmer nights, Lind could manage the massive cedar steering sweep, taller than her five-foot-three frame, by bracing her whole body against it to guide the sailing canoe by the stars.

Other nights the crew could do little to counter. "Sometimes the noise was so much you'd have hallucinations," says Lind. "Total, twenty-four hours a day absolute incredible constant noises—whistles, screams, howling."

Lind recalls the "horrid nightmares," and that she was not the only one having them. The wild conditions, "waves sometimes a couple stories high," were wearing on Tocher, then fifty-one, as well as stressing the steering sweep.

The sweep was grinding on the side of the canoe—wood on wood—and staying on course was becoming a problem. The rudder needed repair. In mid-June, they pulled into Santa Cruz, California. Having a fall semester to begin preparing for, Lind opted to return to B.C., as Tocher fixed the sweep, filling her seat with an intrepid forty-year-old Canadian *Reader's Digest* writer named Richard Tomkies who was covering the expedition. As June ended, the new three-man crew headed south, back into the Pacific.

Twenty-nine days later, the *Orenda*—an Iroquois word meaning an empathy of spiritual power, or a unity in the world—arrived in Waikiki. It was not without hardship. Their radios failed. They had only three days of clear skies. Tocher was suffering through a kidney infection and had to handcraft six spare rudders during the voyage. Tomkies, jumping into his first open-ocean trip ever, described the experience to local press as "sheer terror interspersed with moments of boredom," while Kiesel, the more experienced hand, talked about not wanting the journey to end, calling it "the ultimate challenge."

When the canoe arrived below Diamond Head on July 29, 1978, Lind, who had flown in to Oahu, motored out to greet the crew. Tocher dove in to the warm waters to swim over to her boat.

"Love will make you do many things," explains Lind, who is now the only surviving member of the crew. She still lives walking distance from the West Vancouver launch and has never wanted to sail since; doesn't even feel comfortable on ferries, thank you very much. "It does leave a mark on one," Lind says, "and makes you realize and appreciate and respect out there."

Tocher tried for years to recoup costs, which he cited at close to $60,000, by traveling to show a film he produced from the experience called *The Odyssey of Orenda*. When asked to justify the costs to a reporter, during the layover in Santa Cruz, Tocher struggled to articulate the draw of, as Lind put it, "out there."

"I'm so close to the project, I can't explain the compulsion," he said. "Its justification comes in the empathy of the people who get tangled up with it."

The people who get tangled up—the Hands, the Brintons, the Tochers, the Siglers and Gores, the Quesnels, and the Gillets—they all can empathize. They understand what is wrapped in the compulsion. By Quesnel's math, it all adds up to "99 percent BS and 1 percent adventure."

But that 1 percent amplifies itself profoundly across time. It is that intangible something that settles into the core of who the individuals are who tangle with the crossing. And that something else comes back with instant recall.

That night alone, on the oars, thirty-foot waves "sounding like locomotives crashing around in that cockleshell of a boat," Quesnel knew his situation was dangerous, but within his abilities. Cold, jaw numb from chatter, wet, drenched, tired, and hungry. "You just get this real animalistic, brutal, animal-like attitude of defiance. Nothing can stop you. Is that all you can do? Drop the temperature another degree. Hit me with your best shot. I don't care, I'll make it."

There's only one way to label this elevation in raw self-reliance, as Quesnel calls it: "That absolute savage pride in your ability to survive physical hardship."

CHAPTER THIRTEEN

Guiding Lives

As an experienced wilderness backpacker, Douglas Montgomery knew a bit about the benefits of coping with physical challenge. Let Mother Nature pull your threads and you might learn something. After dabbling in kayak touring around San Francisco Bay, he noticed an ad in a 1996 copy of *Sea Kayaker* magazine.

It pictured a buzzard on a cactus with plain verbiage: For paddlers who wouldn't dream of going on paid tours. Montgomery called up the number for Southwest Kayaks Expeditions and spoke to Kampe about reserving a spot on an expedition and booked a flight to Loreto, two-thirds of the way down the Sea of Cortez side of the Baja California peninsula.

"I didn't want safe," Montgomery said. "I wanted somebody who'd take me to interesting places and that I would learn from."

What Montgomery got was Ed Gillet. When he met his trip leader, Montgomery wasn't sure what to think. Here was a subdued, wiry character with a mop of orange hair, looking "like he was about to get skin cancer." Gillet had just driven a group of kayakers down from San Diego. Montgomery had no idea about Gillet's crossing to Hawaii, nine years prior, or any of the obvious damage that the sun exposure would have left.

And as the group began its multiday circumnavigation of Isla del Carmen, the lessons Gillet began to teach Montgomery had nothing to do with Ed Gillet or his storied expedition career, and certainly never a mention of his Hawaii experience. Montgomery, none the wiser, was still learning to store food in hatches and to move a loaded sea kayak. When the group waited for its slowest paddler, calling the circumnavigation into question, Montgomery confided in Gillet that he was starving.

Montgomery laughs at Gillet's deadpan response: "He said, 'Well, this is how you learn,'" noting how much the words sank in. Montgomery understood he was responsible for his own comfort: He never paddled without food on his deck, within easy reach, ever again. "[Gillet] was a patient and excellent teacher," he said, "mixing the right amount of urgency with the right amount of patience."

On a return trip, Montgomery invited along a friend, who experienced the urgent side during an open-water crossing. When caught in a compromising position, Gillet delivering a necessary on-water directive—one part technique-based instruction, one part pep talk with no words minced. "He said, 'If you don't start paddling, you will get sucked out to sea and die!'"

Montgomery returned for more. Year after year, he signed up for another of Gillet's no-frills offerings, hungry for another tough-love tutorial. That, and because "it was so cheap!"

"I don't think he realized what his experience and knowledge were worth, when you compare his tours with what guiding and experience that others were getting," Montgomery said. "He was so humble with his business and it worked for him, because he felt like he wasn't doing anything: He carried the map and the first aid kit. You set up your tent, you cook your own meal, you set up your boat, you paddle your boat. He just drove and paid for gas. It was like $50 a day, so for a ten-day trip, he was excited for $500 a day."

"I don't believe he made any money," said Bob Licht who, at that time in the late '90s, had been organizing and guiding Baja expeditions for twenty years. "And I don't think he was doing it for that. He loved being in Baja so much that he would get people to pay just enough to pay his way."

Gillet, who admitted he became a "somewhat reluctant guide," would agree with that assessment: the solo adventurer suddenly saddled with flock of ducklings, "leading a parade" to the desolate coastlines where he once used to escape from other people. "But I love to travel and I love to paddle, so this was the perfect job for me," he said, reaffirming his actions with their educational value. "I justified what I was doing by believing that I was teaching my clients the skills they could use to do their own trips."

The leading-leaders approach paid off with Montgomery, who progressed from protected tours in the Sea of Cortez with Gillet to exposed Pacific crossings to California's Channel Islands. Beyond paddling techniques, the things that he soaked up—"little stream of consciousness things you pick up from paddling alongside an expert"—propelled Montgomery to twenty years of launching over fifty of his own expeditions in every corner of the globe, from Madagascar to the Aleutians, across the Baltic and North Sea, to Croatia, Venezuela, Argentina, and Fiji.

"His main influence was assuring me that it didn't have to be dangerous to go out over long mileage over the sea," Montgomery said. "Without Ed Gillet, the idea of a crossing would have never occurred to me."

Gillet was doing a lot that was not occurring to others, which included
outfitters. He came up with thirty multiday trips, some as long as 130
miles taking two weeks to complete. No support boats, no first timers, no
kids. "I couldn't do the sorts of guided kayak trips that might be safest for
clients, take the real adventure out of the trip, and still live with myself,"
Gillet said. "If I were going to lead kayak trips—they would be real."

"It was all very loose," Licht said. "He was always the leader and it was
very communal, participatory, noncommercial. All great, I was just more
into straighter, more commercial trips, but he was doing it differently. He
was going down and doing outrageous stuff."

Most any sea kayak outfitter would label an open-coast tour as outrageous. Guiding outside of a protected archipelago into hazardous rough
water is one thing. Doing it while attending to a group sized over four to
five paddlers? Blasphemy.

Dieter Tremp, a repeat client, was on board as one of twelve paddlers
on a trip where Gillet singlehandedly guided his favorite Baja stretch: the
fifty miles running down the wild, surf-swept Pacific coast south from the
Punta Banda peninsula, near Ensenada, with clear afternoon breezes at
your back, typically.

On the third day, screaming blasts of wind had Gillet rally the group.
They needed to stick together around the point, aiming to paddle behind
the headland to avoid the sudden squall. Tremp, with enough sea kayaking experience to lead the group, paddled confidently close around the
headland. There, thirty-knot downdrafts pushed off refracted water "like
you clap your hands in the tub." Eight-foot peaks pitched up around him
"like the world was breaking loose." Without having recalled even rolling
over, Tremp was in the water, shot straight out of his spraydeck-sealed
cockpit, "the water roiling enough that it broke off my kayak's rudder."
Amidst the heaving peaks, Gillet appeared: "My savior, paddling up like
he was sitting in a pool." What Gillet did next—corralling both Tremp
and his loose kayak, getting him back into his boat, bailing out water, and

sealing him back in to start paddling again—Tremp credits as nothing short of saving his life.

During the rescue, the rest of the group drifted past Gillet and Tremp, downwind, beyond the protected lee of headland. Gillet, in triage mode, needed to chase. "Paddle for your life," he told Tremp. "Try to get to land." After an hour of tortured strokes, exhausted against the wind, with no rudder, Tremp landed through the surf and "did a real Robinson Crusoe where I kissed the sand."

The rest of the group eventually improvised their own crash surf landings, Gillet catching up to the paddlers farthest downwind to usher them in. Spread out along miles of empty beach, the group finally reunited, "nothing broken, no one hurt," for an evening of wild weather and vivid stories traded about each paddler's momentary grapple with desperation.

"I enjoy seeing people reach into themselves and dig down deep and find that resilience to do those trips," Gillet said. "I'm not sure if that's sadistic but I think that's beneficial: doing committing things in order [for them] to do what they didn't think they could."

The things that Tremp did on that 1999 trip—the puckering moment of reckoning at the point, the survival strokes through the surf—certainly left their mark on Tremp's psyche. So much so, that he returned for three more trips with Gillet.

"I felt like with him I was in good hands with a veteran," Tremp said. "He was doing it because he loved paddling, not being the center of attention. It was not his gig to sing at the fire . . . he's not the *Kumbaya* type.

"His real love was the solitary paddling thing and his experience guiding was not wanting to worry about the guests' comfort in their sleeping bags or being squeamish about the breakers or something like that," Tremp added. "I feel like he loved being alone. He'd set up camp and then off he would go in his wet suit to go spearfishing or go abalone diving and then come back with three groupers and provide for dinner."

"He is a brilliant, wonderful person," Tremp concluded, "but I felt like guiding is not what he wanted to do."

The fourteen years of guiding added up: Katie managing the shop, Ed spending two weeks and an estimated fifteen hundred miles out of every month running trips and driving shuttles up and down Baja's lone paved

Mexico Federal Highway 1. With followings of hard-core contingents of clients like Tremp and Montgomery, Gillet continued leading his "squad of ducklings" over big crossings and on risky circumnavigations, never worrying about acquiring commercial permits, and constantly developing "the most difficult things I thought I could get away with."

At times, it felt like he was compromising his self-directed values, taking strangers to still-pristine, oft-traveled pockets of the desolate peninsula. Other times he recognized how much he enjoyed showing people *how* to experience the wild places that mattered—pushing personal boundaries, teaching respect, empowering competence. Guiding, in a true sense.

There was one final milestone in his home waters: linking Southern California's Channel Islands chain. At the end of the 2001 summer season, he launched from Gaviota, west of Santa Barbara, planning to head south and then east, completing lengthy open-water crossings to "hop" along the six main islands open to the public, then sneak an illegal stealth landing on the navy-controlled San Clemente Island, and finally head southeast, straight home to San Diego County.

On September 11 Gillet watched the sun rise like any other day over Santa Cruz Island. He purposely didn't pack a radio, wanting to "be away," tending to that incessant itch that could only be scratched offshore, on the Pacific alone. Landing on Anacapa Island on the afternoon of 9-11, he overheard national park rangers talking about the historic events of the day. After calling Katie to digest the news, he decided to cut the expedition short. With the military on high alert, the appeal of eluding the navy to spike out under a camo ghillie net had lost its appeal. Gillet celebrated his fiftieth birthday paddling in to Oceanside, leaving the completion of the bucket-list trip for another year, if ever. He was ready for a new phase of guiding and life.

He and Kampe closed the shop later that year and Gillet went back on the academic path he had veered off twenty years prior, finishing a master's in rhetoric and writing. He wrote down his paddling experiences from Chile to Hawaii to Baja, framed in T. S. Eliot quotes and Latin references in an account that he shelved, appropriately titled "Paddle or Die." He started teaching high schoolers "whole hog," with challenging

AP course work, two hundred-plus students, and began working on curriculum and staff development at the district level. How to paddle became how to read; how to traverse a place became how to enjoy a story, on a different journey, from A to B.

"Introducing people to some really special aesthetic experience is something I enjoy and it carried over from what we did as guided kayak trips in Baja to teaching," Gillet said.

As he leaned into a heavy workload, Gillet moved on psychologically from the Hawaii crossing. And even from paddling in general. They raffled off the weathered carbon paddles and sold the trusty Tofino. After knocking off the full Channel Islands trip in 2005, he tapered off the distance trips altogether and even sold his surf kayaks. Weekend hiking and mountain biking became the norm. Kampe moved into forensic accounting work for a temp agency and, after a string of unfortunate injuries that sidelined her from Gillet's getaways, began a protracted battle with thyroid cancer.

Gillet first took my call at one of her screening appointments in the summer of 2013. He had some time to kill. Sure, he could talk about the crossing. The vision quest, once a test of self so profound that it was off-limits to his closest paddling partners, was open for a little inquiry. Enough time has passed. "The trip was just something I did," he shrugged.

When I asked how deep the experience cut, Gillet watched a coffee cart go by. It took him straight to the kayak. Right back to Day 55, deck bag with stove kit and coffee stash long gone, woozy from physical exhaustion and Halcion fatigue. He could still taste the crusted coffee remnants that he desperately rehydrated from the Styrofoam cup he found floating by.

These were the type of flashbacks that he didn't mind revisiting—ones that let him appreciate the little things in life. And though Gillet suffered no long-term physical injuries or scars from the Hawaii experience, he said that it still remained a "huge part of my inner consciousness."

—◆—

As I covered the errant 2012 and 2013 expeditions of Vidmar, Biles, and Hand for *Canoe & Kayak*—cataloging a trio of initial attempts that never got past Day 1—I started realizing how much it was Gillet, and what exactly was going on in his inner consciousness, that was the real story. Later that summer, he invited me over to his modest San Diego home to find out.

Sitting in his living room, beneath a large painting on the mantel depicting the endless whitecaps of a dark and choppy sea, he told me about how it was there that he learned his limit.

The only way that he could explain the parameters of that edge was with a grainy video clip. Gillet recognized it immediately in the eyes of Andrew McAuley, another driven adventurer who brought a mountaineering mindset to his 2007 quest to paddle a stock kayak from Australia to New Zealand. His tragic disappearance in the Tasman Sea—just a day shy of completing the expedition after a month of punishing paddling—was well documented, as rescuers recovered his kayak with some of his camera footage intact. The diary-like, point-of-view recordings captured McAuley's tortured inner monologue in a way that Gillet's journal never could.

"You can see it," Gillet said. "He has the camera on him and he films himself and says, 'Fuck this, I'll never do this again,' then the next breath, he says, 'Yeah, this is a great adventure,' and he's looking around, not even aware of the camera, and he's got this haunted look in his eyes and I just totally see that: being of two minds."

The constant tug between fight and flight, the fine line between misery and exhilaration: Gillet could only describe the experience as being perpetually stuck in this intense plane of "double consciousness."

"I felt really stupid the whole time, selfish trying to pull this off," he said. "But knowing at the same time that this is also an incredible moment. Like you're in this place no one else had been! You're in the middle of the ocean in a kayak! It's like that: incredible! This is so stupid . . . and even with that feeling in that moment, at the same time: OK, I have to keep going, I can't turn around."

We talked into a cool August evening that was exactly twenty-six years to the day after his unexpected landfall in Kahului Harbor. We moved the conversation to his back patio, with a wide-open view south and west, out to the Pacific in the distance. Before we sat down, he went to pull out the one memento from the journey that he still kept close, locked in a fireproof safe. And with his shepherd-lab mix, Lucy, curled at his feet I hung on every word he read from the journal as the sun went down.

It was a scene from century's past, straight from a Joseph Conrad novel, men gathered to hear Marlow tell the tale of his great battle with the sea. Kampe looked tentatively on from the sliding door, holding a glass of red wine. They didn't normally invite people into their home; they didn't talk about this stuff anymore. They had lived the excitement and the pain together.

But as Gillet read from the journal, that sense of double consciousness came right back to vivid life. Day 26: "'Do I feel desperate?'" Gillet asked, pausing to provide some context—"and then I give my position"—before continuing: "'Barometer climbing, so maybe I'm past the trough,' some sort of low pressure. 'I don't know whether to rest, dry out, conserve energy, or paddle out of the hole . . . would consider rescue or ride at this point, but no one in the vicinity.'

"'Feel like I've hung myself and it's going to take another 30 days to die.'"

He paused, staring into the journal, "and then you know what I say after that?" Gillet asked.

"'At least it's warmer.'"

He and Kampe erupted. The laughter told me that Gillet was in on the joke. There was some distance. He could recognize the humor in the rapid oscillation between terror and exhilaration. He could objectively look back at the two overlapping states of being. He could understand the others' attraction to duplicating his crossing as some kind of ultimate test: "People want to go and prove themselves," he later said, "and there's just no way to do that in ordinary life."

He labeled that innate human need to assert the self as "an archetypal quest." It's the same struggle Gillet had long outlined for his students while teaching Jon Krakauer's *Into the Wild*, the story of a solo searcher's final stand in the Alaskan bush, revealing deeper conflicts of man versus nature, and more critically of man against self.

This is not an A-to-B journey. That act of reckoning, of going when "every fiber in your body says turn around," has a timeless appeal. Gillet himself admitted that he spent years trying to re-create that experience, taking guests with him to that place where they confront limitations.

Other long-distance ocean paddlers describe similar feelings. In early 2017, after Chris Bertish finished his ninety-three-day, 4,050-mile paddle-powered crossing of the Atlantic, he relived the experience in a sit-down interview and I immediately heard him drift back to that sense of double consciousness. Though he benefited from a custom $100,000, twenty-foot craft, allowing him to claim the crossing as the first completed by paddling standing up, the solo unsupported transit from Morocco to Antigua was not without extreme hardship.

After twelve-hour days of paddling, Bertish could not fully extend his six-foot frame in the sleeping cavity. Not that he was sleeping during nights of thirty-knot winds early in the trip that bashed waves into him sideways. Neck cramped over, all the South African big-wave surfer could do was guess, brace, and wait for the next terrifying explosion of craft-breaking sound in the darkness. Drained physically, he explained the challenge of keeping his head together for the start of a new day of exertion while assessing hull damage simultaneously: "Shit, I need to get up and sponge out my craft while I'm sinking, and, oh, is my hatch taking in how much water? Am I listing on one side? I think I'm listing on one side," he recounted. "Mentally your mind is going, 'Oh, my god, I'm sinking and I am taking on water.' Then you look at your forecast—Am I going to be able to check my hatch in another six days' time? Will I have sunk by that time? Or not, how far am I from land? And all these things are going through your head all the time and you just are trying to keep it together."

And then in the next thought, the horror has passed, and Bertish shifts into revelry. He immediately went to the bliss of paddling "sheet glass" on a calmer night in warmer climes, "looking up and seeing a canopy of light, stars so bright that you can see them trail on the ocean." He recalled "every star as a panel in the sky reflecting down on the ocean— like watching a tapestry of dancing light on the water . . . so mesmerizingly beautiful, where you can hear as clearly as you can see: whales three to five miles away, paddling quietly and still seeing everything with the phosphorescence lit up all around you just like in *Life of Pi*."

These are the scenes that so few people ever get a chance to see through their own eyes.

Two years after the invitation to his house, I trouble Gillet again for lunch on a café patio overlooking the Pacific. He stares out to the water, looking for whale spouts that might pop up this time of year. When I tell him that I've got more detailed questions about the kayak, his life prior to the crossing, he locks in. Brown eyes hold steady through weathered eyelids narrowed down, ever wary. "OK, what do you got for me?" he asks, proceeding to answer the questions candidly, then asks, "What else?" not letting the conversation slide into chitchat. He certainly doesn't ask me any personal questions in return. I'd already kept him waiting. I could feel his impatience, motorcycle helmet in hand, when he beat me to the meeting, cruising up the South Coast Highway 101 on his sport bike. He still has to weave back home through heavy traffic to walk the dogs before the sun sets on his weekend.

At sixty-four, a nautical ring on his right hand with a wave and a cross, I can't help but think how much gravity Gillet brings to the world of ocean paddling. An iconoclast not seeking anything from anyone, the last of the modern century's original Pacific pioneers, the low-budget, high-exposure travelers that started with Geordie Tocher, with Sigler and Gore in their life raft, and Patrick Quesnel on the oars. These are quests from a different time when individuals would answer a calling for the sake of adventure alone. Expeditions without live Tweets. Journeys without endings. Vessels without quarter.

Chapter Fourteen

Never Before, Never Since

GILLET WOULD SCOFF AT THE SUPERLATIVES THAT DESCRIBE HIM. THE first and only? Well sure, "no gringo has done it," he quips, taking a long view back at the Pacific's great ocean voyages. It was merely "another canoe voyage in the long human history of similar events," Gillet would argue, remarkable only in the modern context of rapid jet-powered travel capable of moving the masses across oceans. Even considering the sheer distance, he sandbags the miles in his understated manner: "It was really miserable," he says.

The antiquated and esoteric means of navigation by celestial body and mathematics, Gillet also now downplays, confident he could have arrived in Hawaii "quite easily" without the requisite equipment. Sure, he would not have known when, or been able to pace himself or ration his supplies accordingly. The knowledge of one's location is simply a luxury, as "there's a certain inevitably of getting to the Hawaiian Islands if you keep that course." Precision in measurement and exact positioning, therefore, is less critical in retrospect, especially given Gillet's three-sight running fix method—more or less a running tally estimated to provide peace of mind on daily speed and distance covered, and ultimately "really just an argument that builds up over days and days and days." The positions gave Gillet a "mental construction" of where he was and where he needed to be on the trajectory. A functional GPS unit would also take away the peculiar thrill of uncertainty—the feeling that "every day was like a surprise" adjusting to ever-changing wind and current.

To Gillet, it was all sort of an experiment, and "as it turns out I had just enough to do it." The results of the experiment are still inconclusive; Gillet guesses that if he attempted the crossing in the same manner ten times, that he would die on five of the attempts. The natural intangibles are too significant with the variance in weather systems and any given misfortune in the chaotic waters immediately offshore. Add to that mix the variables, not only in maintaining sanity in one's mind, but also in the physical basics of dealing with one's body, avoiding injury in the boat, even simply boiling water between one's legs.

Though Gillet deflects the accolades, the ability to perform in great discomfort cannot be denied. Neither can the willingness to bear it alone. To this day, as per records kept by the Ocean Rowing Society and the

Great Pacific Race, Gillet is one of only five other people to have successfully completed solo, human-powered crossings between the North American mainland and Hawaii. Twice as many people (twelve) have walked on the moon. How come so few people have traveled this distance alone? One easy answer is the route itself, covering a remote section of ocean that, as David Burch points out, is "about as far from land as you can get on earth," at around the halfway mark. The larger question is what unique traits separate the Quesnels and Gillets. What exactly allows an internally motivated, understated individual to do so much more with so much less?

First off is the physical, says Peter Suedfeld, a renowned psychology professor and researcher who has spent a decorated career studying how people deal with isolated, confined, and extreme environments. There's the basic need to be hardy enough to sustain the physiological stress. On the mental side, these types of "sociable introvert" adventurers have stable emotional states, which jibes with Gillet's self-proclaimed "love-hate relationship with people," and structuring in a social tether through his years spent leading trips. "There's an internally directed mood state," Suedfeld says, "and they don't tend to have great big ups and downs without any particular reason for it; they are pretty equable."

Another personality characteristic that stood out in Dr. Neil Weston's study of solo round-the world sailors in the Velux 5 Oceans Race was each of the studied individual's "capacity to remain calm and to normalize and to rationalize the situation." The calm leads to reasoned problem solving, thinking "in a very ordered and sequential manner to feel confident and safe in carrying out the action."

Take Quesnel, needing to tie himself in to keep his head above water. Or Gillet's need to attach a homemade spare rudder on Day 9, under duress, immersed in punishing waves, tethered to his kayak stern. He needed to focus to set that pin. To Gillet, he equated the sustained presence needed to that of a multiday, big-wall climb: Make progress in one direction, make camp, wake and repeat.

To Colin Guthrie, that focus on the edge of certainty is "something more heightened." The Canadian sports psychologist identifies the ability to deeply connect with the environment as the trait that allows an Ed Gillet to push the subconscious aside and navigate the chaos.

"It's not really risky to them," Guthrie says, recalling the tale of a sailor he interviewed in his PhD study on round-the-world sailing crews, about having to fix line atop the mast at night. "He said, 'I am part of the boat, I am part of the whole environment. There's a rhythm no one can see but I feel it and that allows me to do things in a way that are quite controlled.'"

To get at that rhythm, both Gillet and one of Suedfeld's astronaut-studying colleagues, Dr. Gloria Leon, lean on a single word: absorption. "Like the act of hiking where it consumes my consciousness," Gillet said of the daily grind of the crossing. Leon, meanwhile, points out situational absorption as a key personality characteristic in her quantitative analysis from Anders Kjærgaard's 260-day solo sailboat circumnavigation of the globe, which states, "The ability to become highly engaged in the beauty and majesty of the environment and, thus, pay less attention to long stretches of boredom and monotony is clearly adaptive for engaging in a long-duration solo voyage."

Absorption is exactly how Sarah Outen put it too. As the first and only woman to have crossed the mid-Pacific solo by human power, west to east—from Japan to Alaska in 2013, Outen's crossing was part of the Brit's impressive 4.5-year, 250,000-mile global circumnavigation by rowboat, kayak, and bicycle. "Sometimes it's just absorbing being out there, surrounded by water, watching and seeing the changing colors," Outen said, describing her mental space on the 150 days alone across the Pacific, staying engaged in the moment. "And sometimes there's huge amounts of concentration needed to keep the boat going or to stay awake or deal with another dilemma which its taking up some mental space."

After fifty days out on his recent Atlantic crossing, Chris Bertish described becoming so immersed in the immediate that he developed a kinship with his craft such that "it almost became an extension of me." With no sail flapping or engine running, Bertish recognized he was traveling at the same speed as his environment. "You're so in synch and flow with the elements that creatures interact with you as one of them and suddenly this new full matrix unfolds that you've never been able to read or see before."

Quesnel, decades prior, had a similar experience. It took him less than two weeks to make a newfound mental breakthrough. "And then it's like you realize the power of your mind and the ability to focus, think deeply about stuff," Quesnel said. "You can look back over your life and be able to focus on your life, who your friends were and who your fake friends were. Looking back things are so much clearer.

"We live our normal eight-to-five life and have so much stuff going through our minds constantly interacting: What am I going to say? What am I going to do? What's that going to be like? And so, you've got this constant clutter over your mind," Quesnel said. "It took me ten days of solitude where that stuff would start working its way out."

With the clutter cleared, those idle thoughts, Sarah Outen says, are not necessarily idle. "Sometimes they are quite active and I think that's the best part of being alone," she said. "Your brain can just explore itself, explore what you're thinking, explore how you're feeling, thoughts about the future, thoughts about the past, or thoughts about nothing just Winnie-the-Pooh-style bits and pieces wandering in or out."

That sense of self-knowledge has been invaluable for Outen, who now books countless motivational speaking engagements. More importantly, it is the act of revisiting that headspace—where she learned what makes her tick, what forms her triggers and her motivators—that is a well of strength.

The minds of these ocean crossers remain so solid, withstanding decades of life challenges, precisely because of just how hard that foundation was tested.

"You read these stories about yourself like some kind of nut, imbalanced and suicidal, the chorus of 'You're gonna die,'" Quesnel says. "But once you break down the brick walls of limitations, you no longer care what anyone thinks of you, which can be a strength. It can also be a weakness, but you just have that deep sincere belief in yourself.

"And that just stays down there for the rest of your life," Quesnel adds. "I'm not afraid of taking risks: changing occupations, if you're not happy, taking whatever actions it takes. That ultimate ironclad belief in yourself is pretty empowering."

That reward, a lifetime's worth of confidence and focus, remains proportionate to what was risked and endured to earn it. This mindset exists because of the misery, the pain, the desolation, the "benevolent solitude" described by Quesnel and experienced by Gillet, stuck in the dead calm of the mid-Pacific, scrawling coordinates on the hull like a prisoner notching days in a cell: "same ocean, different numbers." That, and the spikes of terror. Being of two minds.

Living with that intense daily choice between sanity and madness, straddling sink or swim, isn't easy for most, especially for landlubbers born without the classic traits that Dr. Frank Farley outlined as the Type T (thrill-seeking) personality that might get us offshore. But as Farley posits, risk taking ought to be taught from an early age "as the fourth R."

"People can't handle uncertainty," says Farley, a psychologist at Temple University and former president of the American Psychological Association. "You can either look at uncertainty as a challenge and as fascinating and interesting, or look at it with fear. So it's an impediment to progress."

Farley, like the outlying adventurers he has spent his career crisscrossing the globe to study, is always looking ahead. A future of "incredible change and uncertainty," with challenges to humanity from artificial intelligence to space colonization, he argues, needs more Gillets. They serve as role models capable of "testing human qualities and speaking for the rest of us," by engaging the unknown, and adapting to change.

For the average weekend warrior, that directive doesn't mean crossing an ocean. Rather, Farley simply advocates "shaking up your habits" to stretch the emotional muscles of risk taking: injecting novelty, variety, and intensity into day-to-day life. It doesn't have to be a brush with death to help reel us back to our instinctual selves. Just a push in that direction.

"It's inherently human to push hard," Farley says. "That's what got us here."

Gillet agrees. "It used to be normal to take a wagon trail across the country," he says. "And now we've come more or less to expect comfort and all of our endeavors to be achieved with minimal effort."

To make his point, he relies on a literary reference, a character's line from Cormac McCarthy's *All the Pretty Horses* that jumped out as a truth: "You can take a lot more than you think."

"I might be overly romantic or old school," he says, "but there's a value to connect with those more primal, and more universal, experiences."

Gillet worries about the overscheduled, underexperienced students he helps guide out of high school and into their adult lives. He spends his summers taking steps to continue working, reading for AP tests, pushing the curriculum boundaries. He wants to leave a legacy in the district.

Having asked some of the greatest minds in risk-taking science, they all had one conclusion. They were all equally fascinated by Gillet's journey. Some wished they could study his mind in real time, others wanted to analyze his journal: how he processed risk, how he performed in such extreme discomfort. And still thirty-one years on, no one has come close to surviving a sea kayak voyage as bold. I started wondering about Gillet's legacy. How *did* he do it? How did he reconcile and perform in the crux moments?

Simple, he answered. He stopped and ate. Just like in rock climbing, stuck on the wall. You talk yourself down and do what the situation requires.

"Whenever I would start to feel panicky or think, 'Should I stop the trip, pull the pin on my EPIRB, oh my god,' I would do one practical thing: eat food," says Gillet, noting it was an adage that Ray Jardine passed along. "It's a kind of negative fantasy: all that what if. It is all just coming from some imaginative place," he added. "I dealt with it by just being practical—what do I need to do to move the boat another fifty feet west, and that helped me every time. It didn't matter what it was, maybe it's a game but I don't think it is. I think anxiety in general, making lists, short-term goals, and trying to achieve and not thinking about the next thirty years. I just narrowed my focus down to short-term goals to cope with anxiety.

"In a kayak you have to recognize the situation: You can't drive faster, you can only go the distance, so recognizing the limitations and damping down or dealing with that anxiety . . . that practicality, that realization is the only remedy."

Ed Gillet's recognition of his own limitations is what ultimately allowed him to break through so many that others imposed.

The man who shortened his horizon to go over one is now assessing other limitations, looking at his life journey and career arc. At sixty-six, entering what is likely to be his last year teaching high schoolers, Gillet is ready to let the story go. The last time we talked, over thirty years after he quietly washed up in Maui, he still recognized the problem in him trying to retread the tale, attempting to frame the level of intensity, suffering, and insight. "It just becomes a justification," he says, sensing bits of self-betrayal percolating back to the surface. But now he can also understand the value of other captive adventurers who can view the test through their own experiences alone, up against their own demons: "It makes that connection where you can actually see and imagine what it's like to be out there," he says. "That situational feeling of being as far as you can be from rescue, of being up against it, in a make-it-or-you-don't, life-or-death situation."

There's no more expectation or belief that he can put someone in his position mid-ocean to truly understand. He's ready to recognize the limitation of that anxiety, and let it go. Except he's not. The trip is too tightly wound into his fabric. He told me he journeyed out to the desert to find the Tofino that he had sold off decades ago. The same summer that Necky Kayaks' corporate ownership liquidated the once venerable brand, the industry moving in friendlier directions, Gillet struggled to heave the 130-pound seafaring dinosaur onto his car. Why? He doesn't know what to make of it.

It was never about the kayak. He was simply seeking. The number-one single when Gillet stumbled into the Maui Beach Hotel: U2's *Still Haven't Found What I'm Looking For*. And the tune has not changed. "Whatever it was I was looking for, I'm still looking for it," he says. "There were no answers there. There's no answer."

That doesn't diminish our desire to glimpse what he saw on the other side. Like the students in his classroom or the core of acolytes on his guided trips, regular paddlers seek him out to find something out about themselves—perhaps they might learn something by quietly stepping off the safety of the beach to go and do. They might go farther than they thought.

There is one last open end. Nearing the end of his teaching tenure, and with Kampe's cancer in remission, the couple plans to sell their house, cash out, buy a boat, and sail away. Always moving ahead to the next horizon. After all, Gillet has never ventured beyond Hawaii.

He wants to be perpetually back in that place on the mantel: the sprawling painting of whitecaps on choppy seas. Back to the game of committing to deal with one's body, the ocean, the weather. Adapting and surviving. Back to a place where "space and time change completely and you're in this moment and when the sea lets you go, that's when you get up."

It's in that place, moving at the speed of the elements, where he tapped long-dormant knowledge, gaining an ability to read cues and make the blank landscape as intelligible "as the desert to a Bedouin." Crossing from one point to another is simply a mechanism for that expansion of senses, the destination an anticlimactic return back to the ordinary.

It's in that place where Gillet knows he is merely a tourist in transit, a different type of pelagic creature finding his way. For brief moments, he can still cut loose from the familiar. As only he can put it:

All of us are transients here. What endures is our planet and her oceans. From my mid-Pacific vantage point, human artifice and artifacts appeared small and temporary. This is why dreamers will always build boats to voyage into that eternal ocean realm: to gain the perspective that is hidden from those who stay close to the shore.

Postscript

On, May 1, 2018, R. W. Hand's fourth attempt to re-create Ed Gillet's solo kayak crossing to Hawaii came to an immediate, and near-fatal end. Seventeen hours after Hand's launch from the Monterey Harbor, local surfer Jon Kramer spotted a large tandem kayak, empty in tumultuous waters on the opposite, exposed western side of the Monterey Peninsula. Kramer called 911, located a face-down and motionless Hand (separated from both his life jacket and kayak), and helped pull him from the water with arriving first responders, who performed CPR and successfully returned Hand's pulse before emergency transport to a nearby Monterey hospital. Over the next month at the hospital, Hand made steady progress transitioning from life support through treatments and both speech and physical therapy, as his condition became more stable and he became more responsive. At the time of press, Hand was preparing for air transport to continue recovery in medical care near family in West Texas.

ACKNOWLEDGMENTS

People do not live out their dreams, test their limits, in a vacuum. This book is for the enabler stakeholder foundations of support that people who seek and who push stand upon.

For the people who never get their share of the credit for the weight that they carry.

For my wife, Kristin. I love you forever.

For Katie.

And for River.

To be strong enough to go, to ask, and to seek.

That's what this book is: an attempt to push. To expand as a writer and share the story of a person who has inspired me each time I'm on the water and want to head in, pull out, give up, or turn back because of fatigue or temporary discomfort. Maybe I can go a little farther, maybe I can draw this out a little further. Add another mile, another 100 words, stretch, and see where the story goes.

Thanks to Mel and TJ Lubey for the initial push.

To Dave Costello for that boost of confidence to build the framework.

To Eugene Buchanan for the well-timed advice and encouragement.

To Jeff Moag for a decade of recognizing value in giving my ideas space and shape to grow.

To Parker Meek, Robert Zaleski, Todd Lynch, Aaron Schmidt, Joe Carberry, and Will Taylor: the support of this story, starting from its inception through its realization in the editorial production trenches, has not been forgotten.

Finally to my parents, Patricia and John, for their unending interest in my development and especially my father for his continued interest in every step of this process, every stroke forward.

This book wouldn't have been possible without their help, as well as that of Diana and John Corpstein, and that of Laura and Danny Powers, whose everyday support has been instrumental in our simultaneous attempt to start a family, launch a business, and finish this book.

Index

About the Author

Dave Shively is a Colorado-bred, California-based journalist who serves as the Content Director for TEN: The Enthusiast Network's Paddlesports Group. As the longtime managing editor of *Canoe & Kayak* and senior editor of *SUP* magazine, which he helped launch in 2009, Shively established a respected voice in the sport by grounding unique profiles and travel narratives in paddling experiences documented from Nunavut to New Orleans, and while tracking the rise of stand-up paddleboarding from fjords in Alaska to canals in Venice. Shively recently won Folio's 2017 Single Article Eddie Award for "Healing Waters" (*Canoe & Kayak*, Winter 2016), a series of veteran profiles exploring PTSD and the transformative power of the outdoors.